TURN ME OVER......I'M REVERSIBLE

by
KAYE WOOD

Quick and Easy Reversible Quilts

PRINTED AND DISTRIBUTED BY
EZ INTERNATIONAL / 95 Mayhill St., Saddle Brook, N.J. 07662

TABLE OF CONTENTS

INTRODUCTION
- Why Reversible Quilts 1
- Color in Quilts 1
- Choose your fabric 2
- Quilt batting 2
- Fabric preparation 2
- Marking and cutting accurately 3
- Sewing accurately 3
- Quilting 3
- Equipment 4

CHAPTER I: QUILTS MADE WITH RECTANGLES
- Babyland Crib Quilt 6
- Dimension (Double Bed Size) 9
- Rings of Color (Queen Size) 11
- Amish Bars Baby Quilt 12
- Reaching Fingers (Double Bed Size) 15
- Kaye's Waste Basket Quilt 26

CHAPTER II: QUILTS MADE WITH DIAMOND SHAPES
- Barn Raising (Double Bed Size) 27
- The King of Diamonds (King Size) 30
- Starmaker Wall Hanging 36
- Amish Silhouette Wall Hanging 43

CHAPTER III: REVERSIBLE APPLIQUE
- Silhouette Applique 49
- Broderie Perse 50
- Silhouette Quilting 50

CHAPTER IV: REVERSIBLE CLOTHING 51

CHAPTER V: HOW TO FINISH A QUILT
- Yardage needed 53
- Tying Your Quilt 53
- Borders 54
- Bindings 54

"Turn Me Over — I'm Reversible" is dedicated to Jane Ehinger of West Branch, Michigan. Jane is a student of mine as I am a student of hers. She teaches many forms of hand and machine patchwork and quilting; she also designs many of her own patterns and quilts.

Just a phone call to Jane to talk over a different technique will result in a finished quilt top a few days later. Because of this, Jane is known as "Jane Doe" during my quilting lecture/demonstrations. After all, wouldn't everyone want Jane to keep delivering quilt tops with new ideas.

Jane is an artist with fabric colors; her quilts and wall hangings go with me and are part of my "Log Cabin" and "Starmakers Ablaze" demonstrations.

Thanks to Jane, my students are exposed to a greater variety of patterns and colors to help them in their quiltmaking.

INTRODUCTION
REVERSIBLE QUILTS

Why reversible quilts?
1. In reversible quilting, both sides of the quilted item are sewn and quilted at the same time. No additional quilting is needed. The only hand sewing might be the final step in applying the binding.
2. A reversible quilt can be made in a short amount of time, sometimes just hours. In some cases, the entire quilt can be made in less time than a traditional **quilt top** can be pieced. If you are in the business of selling quilted items, the less time spent on a quality item, the more money per hour you can make.
3. You can color coordinate a quilt for more than one season or holiday.
4. If you have a fabric store, reversible quilts are great for displaying different coordinated fabrics. One side of the quilt can be shown in your window display; the reverse side can face into the shop.
5. A wall divider can be made up of a reversible quilt. Two possible room decors will give added interest with just one quilt.

COLOR IN QUILTS

Color and pattern help to mold the quilt into a pleasing design. Both are important to the "continuity" of your quilt. The patterns used are repeated throughout the quilt either in full or part; or the continuity is accomplished through repeated uses of the same colors.

All colors used in the quilt can be repeated in the borders or the binding. If many colors are used, the appearance of the quilt can sometimes be tied together by repeating each color used at least three times throughout the quilt.

The colors you choose for your patchwork will be influenced by your favorite color combinations, the room in which your patchwork will be displayed, and the standard color combinations.

Clear, or bright, colors look well together. Muddy or muted colors look well together. But be careful of mixing bright and muted colors in the same pattern. Sometimes it works but more often the color combination is not satisfactory.

The same patchwork design can look completely different when different colors are used or when the light and dark fabrics are reversed.

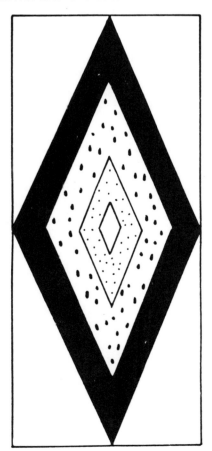 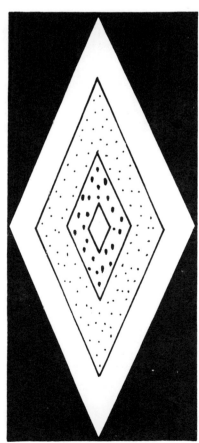

See Chapter 2 for directions.

Dark colors tend to recede into the background, while light colors come forward toward you. Also, dark colored sections tend to look smaller. Look at the two diamond patterns on the previous page. The diamond with the dark center draws your eye into the center of that pattern. In the other diamond, your eye is drawn to the dark outside diamond.

With the reversible quilt, you can make a diamond quilt with the dark center on one side and the light center on the reverse side — a much different effect of color in the same quilt.

Try two different monochromatic color schemes in your reversible quilt. My Rose/Blue quilt has many shades of rose on one side; the reverse side is made up of dusty blues. The binding is made from a printed fabric with both rose and blue in the design.

Or, an interesting quilt would have all neutrals (black, gray, beige, white) on one side; the reverse side could be done in brilliant primary colors.

An interesting wall hanging could be done in Christmas colors on one side; the reverse color scheme could match the room decor. This would be a good idea for a tablecloth, too.

CHOOSE YOUR FABRIC

Fabric for most patchwork patterns should be cotton or a cotton blend. Quilters differ over which they prefer. My preference is for the cotton blends for several reasons:

1. I like the finish on the fabrics.
2. I don't like to iron except when necessary to press seam allowances flat.
3. Blends are more durable and color fast than 100% cottons.
4. Blends do not stretch during sewing and handling; 100% cottons sometimes do, particularly when working with long strips, such as borders and bindings.

But, I make my choice mainly by color and not by fabric content.

When working with some of the diagonally cut patterns, such as the stars, it is much easier to work with similar fabrics, e.g., all cottons or all blends.

When using printed fabrics, be aware of the size of the print in relation to the size of the pattern. Large prints should be avoided in small pieced areas.

Color coordination in fabrics is easier within one company's color line. The blues made by one fabric company are more likely to coordinate with other blues from that same company. Some of the companies have come out with an entire line of color coordinated fabrics. If your favorite fabric or quilt store carries a completely coordinated line, it will help your fabric selection.

QUILT BATTING

For the reversible quilts, I prefer to use Mountain Mist Fatt Batt™ by Stearns and Foster. It has a high loft and is perfect for machine stitching.

Fatt Batt™ will give you more of a comforter look. If you prefer a flatter quilt, use a light weight batting or fleece.

The batting should be cut in lengthwise strips. Fatt Batt™ has a lot of stability and will keep its shape if cut lengthwise. The batting can be cut with the rotary cutter or with shears.

FABRIC PREPARATION

Fabric should be machine washed and dried. This will remove the sizing and takes care of any possible shrinkage. If the dyes in the fabric are not colorfast, it is better to find out now than after your quilt is finished. If necessary, press the fabric before cutting.

Before washing, cut diagonally across each corner of the piece of fabric. This will prevent ravelling during washing and drying. Also, if you get into the habit of always making this diagonal cut immediately before washing fabric, you will always know if a piece of fabric is ready to use, even if it sits on your fabric shelf for months.

If the corners are cut off, the piece of fabric has been washed and dried.

MARKING AND CUTTING ACCURATELY

Most of the patchwork patterns in this book involve working with long strips of fabric. The strips are usually cut across the width (44/45") of the fabric, from selvage to selvage. It is important that these strips be cut straight.

Fold the fabric in half, right sides together, selvage edges together. Then fold the fabric again, bringing the first fold to the selvage edges. Your fabric will now be in four layers.

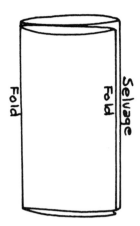
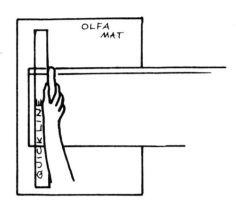

Lay the folded fabric on the Olfa Cutting Mat. Use a heavy plastic ruler, such as the Nancy Crow Quickline ruler. Pull the Olfa Rotary Cutter along the edge of the Quickline ruler. The Rotary Cutter will cut up to 8 layers of fabric at a time.

The Quickline ruler has markings for widths from ¼" up to 3 inches.

Double check the width of your strips by laying cut strips on top of each other. It is easier to recut a few strips now than to have seams not line up and finished squares be uneven because of strips cut inaccurately.

SEWING ACCURATELY

A ¼" seam allowance is used in all of the reversible quilts in this book.

If your sewing machine **needle** is not ¼" from the **edge** of the presser foot, you have two choices:

1. Use the width of the presser foot for your seam allowance consistently. Your seam allowance will then be narrower or wider than ¼". Your quilted item will be slightly smaller or larger than the finished size given in this book, but you should not have any other problems because of this.

2. Change the needle position, if possible, so that the distance from the needle to the edge of the presser foot is exactly ¼". On my Viking 980, I have to move my needle two positions to the right to have an exact ¼" seam.

When making samples for this book, I did change the needle position to give me ¼". I needed to do this so my samples would be the same as the instructions in the book. However, when I make reversible quilts for my own use or for gifts, I just use the seam allowance that I get from using the centered needle position, which is about ⅜".

I also use a magnetic seam guide, made by Dritz, on my machine. I place the lipped edge against the edge of my presser foot. Then the fabric feeds through the machine right against the seam guide. It is much easier than always watching to make sure that the fabric is exactly even with the edge of the presser foot.

QUILTING

The quilting is all done on the machine as the strips are added. Therefore no hand or machine quilting will show on reversible quilts.

However, on some of the larger pieces, hand or machine quilting, hand or machine tying, or a combination of stenciling and quilting may be done. Stenciling would be done before adding the piece to the quilt. Quilting would be done after the entire quilt is finished.

Kaye Wood's
THE QUILT LIKE A PRO PROGRAM

a total and continuous program of
FASTER — EASIER — MORE ACCURATE
MACHINE PATCHWORK
NO TEMPLATES USED

BOOKS
by Kaye Wood

"QUILT LIKE A PRO"
A basic strip piecing manual; over 1,000 diagrams; including squares, half-squares, diamonds, stars, Seminole, Log Cabin patterns, quilted clothing, finishing techniques.

"TURN ME OVER - I'M REVERSIBLE"
Completely reversible quilts; unique 3-layer quilting process.

"SERGER PATCHWORK PROJECTS"

"STARMAKERS ABLAZE I"
Strip pieced Log Cabin triangles made easy enough for beginners; full color.

"STARMAKERS ABLAZE II"
Strip pieced Log Cabin diamonds are fast and easy; full color.

"STRIP QUILTING PROJECTS"
12 projects shown on the PBS-TV series "Strip Quilting".

"STRIP QUILTING PROJECTS 2"
Projects from the "STRIP QUILTING 2" series as shown on PBS-TV stations.

TOOLS
by Kaye Wood

STARMAKER 5
Perfect 5-pointed stars; 20-piece Dresden Plates; Seminole Patchwork; "Quilt Like A Pro" and "Serger Patchwork Projects", and "Strip Quilting Projects".

STARMAKER 6
Perfect 6-pointed stars, spiderwebs, tumbling blocks, Seminole, Log Cabin triangles and diamonds. Used in all of the books.

STARMAKER 8
Perfect 8-pointed stars, diamonds, Dresden plates, Seminole and Log Cabin diamonds. Used in "Quilt Like A Pro", Turn Me Over - I'm Reversible" and "Serger Patchwork Projects", and "Strip Quilting Projects".

VIEW-A-STRIP
View fabric as it will look in patchwork from 1" to 3" wide.

VIDEO TAPES
by Kaye Wood

BASIC LOG CABIN
from "Quilt Like A Pro"

LOG CABIN TRIANGLES
from "Starmakers Ablaze, Volume 1"

REVERSIBLE QUILTS
from "Turn Me Over - I'm Reversible

LOG CABIN DIAMONDS
from "Starmakers Ablaze II"

STAMAKERS QUILT DESIGNS
using the Starmakers Tools

A BOOK IS BORN

It was Spring 1983. Sally Eustice, owner of Sally's Fabrics in Cheboygan, Michigan, and I were asked to design a marketable product for a cottage industry.

This product had to be:

> marketable
> fast
> requiring minimal sewing skills
> able to be done at home
> priced to bring at least a minimum wage.

How could we find such a product?

First, what could the two of us do? Patchwork and quilting are what we knew best. We have both taught sewing and quilting, and Sally had a fabric store. So — down to her store to pick out five yards each of black, gray and white polished cotton.

Then came the RESEARCH. We stopped at a waterbed store because it was on our way and we just happened to drive by. The quilts on the beds were mostly log cabin strip style patterns. "Why couldn't these designs be made reversible like the reversible log cabin in my book **"QUILT LIKE A PRO"**?

Finally came the BRAINSTORMING — all evening and most of the night. Pepsi kept us going. Fabric covered the floor of Sally's living room.

The first sample took us about five hours. I diagrammed, designed; we both cut fabrics and quilt batting; Sally sewed. The strips were not always cut straight; the fabric didn't always catch in the seam on the underside, and the binding was not yet on the quilt — but that's OK — the design grew, techniques developed, and mistakes led to eventual changes.

AND in one day and one night, the book,
"TURN ME OVER . . . I'M REVERSIBLE"
was conceived
and is now born!

Happy Birthday!

P.S. My black, gray and white reversible quilt is still without a binding and the edges are not all caught in the seams. It will probably never be finished because it reminds me of the creative processes that became **"Turn Me Over . . . I'm Reversible."** (Those of you who know me also know there are other reasons why it will never be finished.)

No matter what quilting represents to you — a hobby or perhaps a cottage industry — I am sure you will enjoy this brain-child that grew out of Sally's and my original idea.

CHAPTER I

BABYLAND CRIB QUILT

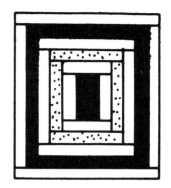

Finished size: 30" x 36"

Fabric needed: 3 yards

Binding: ⅓ yard Fatt Batt™

You can't miss with pinks for one side and blues for the reverse side. Or choose pastel greens and yellows. Try it in shades of all one color — start with a dark center and gradually get lighter on one side. The reverse can start with a light center and gradually get darker.

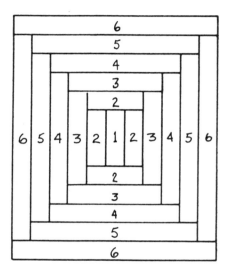

FABRIC REQUIREMENTS

Position #		Buy	Cut
1 (center)	Side A	¼ yard	6" x 12"
	Side B	¼ yard	6" x 12"
	Batting		6" x 12"
2	Side A	¼ yard	2 strips 3" x 45"
	Side B	¼ yard	2 strips 3" x 45"
3	Side A	¼ yard	2 strips 3" x 45"
	Side B	¼ yard	2 strips 3" x 45"
4	Side A	⅓ yard	4 strips 3" x 45"
	Side B	⅓ yard	4 strips 3" x 45"
5	Side A	⅓ yard	4 strips 3" x 45"
	Side B	⅓ yard	4 strips 3" x 45"
6	Side A	⅓ yard	4 strips 3" x 45"
	Side B	⅓ yard	4 strips 3" x 45"
	Fatt Batt™		as needed 3" x 45" (batting — cut lengthwise)
	Binding	⅓ yard	4 strips 3" x 45"

Step 1: Make a chart of the colors you will use in each position. This will help in planning both sides of your quilt and will keep the strips of color in order.

Cut fabric swatches (or write a description of the fabric); glue or tape them in place opposite the "Position #" column under "Side A" and "Side B."

Side A	Position #	Side B
_____	1 (center)	_____
_____ fabric	2	_____ fabric
_____ swatches	3	_____ swatches
_____	4	_____
_____	5	_____
_____	6	_____

Step 2: Make a quilt sandwich from center (position #1) fabric:

    6" × 12" Side A on one side of 6" × 12" batting;

    6" × 12" Side B on reverse side; the wrong side of fabric against the quilt batting.

Pin all three layers together.

Set machine for medium wide zigzag and long stitch length.

Zigzag all four sides.

You now will have a 6" × 12" finished rectangle that will form the center of your quilt.

SIDE B WILL ALWAYS BE UNDERNEATH AS NEW STRIPS ARE ADDED.

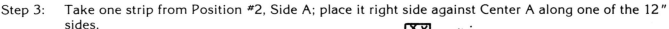

Step 3: Take one strip from Position #2, Side A; place it right side against Center A along one of the 12" sides.

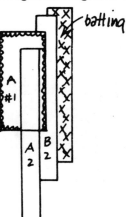

Place strip from Position #2, Side B, right side against Center B.

Lay a strip of quilt batt against the wrong side of the B strip.

Pin all four layers together.

Sew with ¼" seam allowance.

Trim excess quilt batting from the seam allowance.

Open out Position #2 (both fabrics and quilt batting).

Pin all three edges together carefully.

Trim the ends of the A and B strips even with the center.

Zigzag the open edges together.

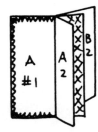

Step 4: Add position #2 strips Side A and Side B to the opposite side of the center rectangle (#1).

Keep the B strip on the bottom with the quilt batt against the wrong side of the B strip.

Pin all four layers together.

Sew at ¼" seam allowance.

Trim quilt batt from seam allowance.

Open out position #2 strips.

Pin all three layers together.

Trim ends of strips and batt even with center rectangle.

Zigzag edges together.

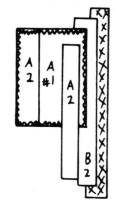 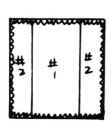

— 7 —

Step 5: Add position #2 strips Side A and Side B to the top and bottom of the center rectangle (#1).

Keep the Side B strip on the bottom with the quilt batt against the wrong side of the B strip.

Pin all four layers together.
Sew at ¼" seam allowance.
Trim quilt batt.
Open out position #2 strips.
Pin together; trim ends of strips;
zigzag edges together.

Step 6: Continue adding strips from positions #3 through #6 in the same way.

Always add the strips to the sides first; then to the top and bottom.

Zigzag the outside edges of the quilt (strips #6).

Step 7: Put the binding on following the directions in the Chapter on Finishing Quilts.

VARIATIONS:

Try some of these ideas:

* Start with a fabric with a nursery print for the center rectangle. If any quilting is to be done around a portion of the print, it should be done after Step 2.
* Stencil a design into the center rectangle. This should be done before **Step 2**.
* Make your quilt with a Log Cabin Court House Steps design: dark strips on two opposite sides of the center rectangle; light strips on the other two opposite sides.
* Put a reverse silhouette applique in the center. See Chapter III.

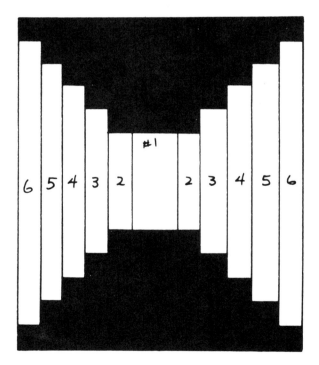

Side A

Side B could have the dark strips on the sides and the light strips at the top and bottom of the center rectangle.

DIMENSION (Double Bed Size)

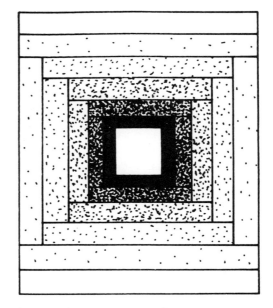

Finished size: 68" x 85"
Fabric needed: 6½ yards each side
Binding: ¾ yard Fatt Batt™

The center of this design is 8" x 8", large enough to make it a center of interest.

Do you have an interesting lace design? Applique the lace to side A. The applique can be done before the center quilt sandwich is put together. Quilting can then be done, if desired, after the center is together; just the quilting lines will show on Side B.

If you need to make the center larger, just eliminate some of the strips that form a border for the center.

You may want to repeat the center motif on the outside borders, either #6 strip which goes completely around the center, or #7 strip which is only added to the top and bottom.

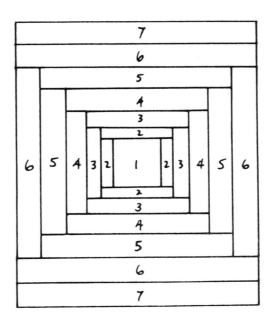

— 9 —

FABRIC REQUIREMENTS

Position #		Buy	Cut
1 (center)	Side A	¼ yard	8" × 8"
	Side B	¼ yard	8" × 8"
	Batting		8" × 8"
2	Side A	⅛ yard	1 strip 3" × 45"
	Side B	⅛ yard	1 strip 3" × 45"
3	Side A	⅓ yard	2 strips 5" × 45"
	Side B	⅓ yard	2 strips 5" × 45"
4	Side A	1 yard	4 strips 7" × 45"
	Side B	1 yard	4 strips 7" × 45"
5	Side A	1⅔ yards	6 strips 9" × 45"
	Side B	1⅔ yards	6 strips 9" × 45"
6	Side A	2 yards	8 strips 9" × 45"
	Side B	2 yards	8 strips 9" × 45"
7	Side A	1 yard	4 strips 9" × 45"
	Side B	1 yard	4 strips 9" × 45"

Cut batting strips lengthwise as needed.

Make a chart showing the colors you want to use for each side of the quilt.

Side A	Position #	Side B
_____	1 (center)	_____
_____	2	_____
_____	3	_____
_____	4	_____
_____	5	_____
_____	6	_____
_____	7	_____

Add the strips and batting to the center square in the same way as shown in the Babyland Crib Quilt. Position #7 is only added to the top and bottom of the quilt.

RINGS OF COLOR

Finished size: 83" x 98" (queen size)

Fabric needed: 7 yards each side

Binding: ¾ yard Fatt Batt™

 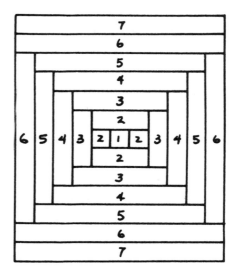

FABRIC REQUIREMENTS

Position #		Buy	Cut
1 (center)	Side A	¼ yard	8" x 8"
	Side B	¼ yard	8" x 8"
	Batting		8" x 8"
2	Side A	½ yard	2 strips 8" x 45"
	Side B	½ yard	2 strips 8" x 45"
3	Side A	1 yard	4 strips 8" x 45"
	Side B	1 yard	4 strips 8" x 45"
4	Side A	1⅓ yards	6 strips 8" x 45"
	Side B	1⅓ yards	6 strips 8" x 45"
5	Side A	2 yards	8 strips 8" x 45"
	Side B	2 yards	8 strips 8" x 45"
6	Side A	2 yards	8 strips 8" x 45"
	Side B	2 yards	8 strips 8" x 45"
7	Side A	1 yard	4 strips 8" x 45"
	Side B	1 yard	4 strips 8" x 45"

Make a chart showing the colors you want to use.

Side A	Position #	Side B
_____	1 (center)	_____
_____	2	_____
_____	3	_____
_____	4	_____
_____	5	_____
_____	6	_____
_____	7	_____

Follow instructions for adding strips given in the Log Cabin Baby Quilt.

AMISH BARS BABY QUILT

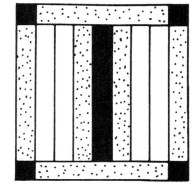

Finished size: 38" × 48"

Fabric needed: 3½ yards

Binding: ⅓ yard

Fatt Batt™: 38" × 48"

The Amish Bar pattern is traditionally made with all solid colors. You may want to make a summer quilt (light colors) on Side A and a winter quilt (dark colors) on Side B.

FABRIC REQUIREMENTS

Inside Bars	Side A	7 strips 4" × 36"
	Side B	7 strips 4" × 36"
Borders	Side A	4 strips 6" × 36"
	Side B	4 strips 6" × 36"
Border Squares	Side A	1 strip 6" × 24"
	Side B	1 strip 6" × 24"
Fatt Batt™		Cut lengthwise in 4" and 6" wide strips
Binding	⅓ yard	4 strips 3" × 45"

Step 1: Make a chart showing the colors you want to use for each side of the quilt.

Side A	Position #	Side B
_____	1 (center)	_____
_____	2	_____
_____	3	_____
_____	4	_____
_____	5	_____
_____	6	_____
_____	7	_____
_____	Border strips	_____
_____	Border squares	_____

Write in the colors on the chart opposite the position #.

Step 2: Make a quilt sandwich from position #1: Side A strip on one side of the quilt batting; Side B strip on the other side of the batting; the wrong side of the fabric against the quilt batting.
Pin all edges together; Zigzag all four edges close to the edge of the fabric.
Check to see that the fabric on Side A and Side B is all caught in the zigzag stitch.

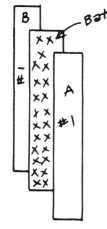

Step 3: Side B will always be underneath as new strips are added.

Lay the strip for position #2, Side A right side down against Side A, position #1. Lay the strip for #2, Side B, right side up against #1, Side B. Lay the quilt batting strip under Side B strip.

Pin all the pieces together carefully.
Stitch at ¼".

Open out the position #2 strips. Pin the edges together carefully. Zigzag around all edges.

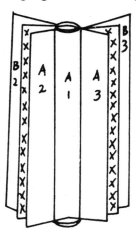

Step 4: Add the strips for position #3 through #7 in the same way.

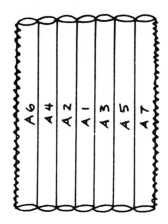

Step 5: Add the top and bottom border strips by placing the border strip A right side down against the A side of the quilt; border strip B right side against the B side of the quilt; 6" strip of batting underneath border strip B.

Open out the border strips; pin the edges carefully. Trim the ends of the border strips and quilt batting even with the outside of the quilt.

Zigzag all edges closed.

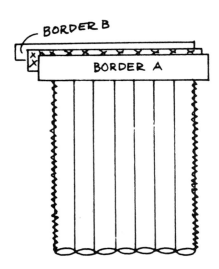
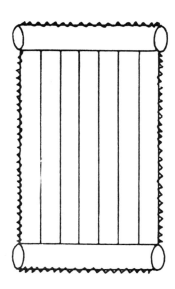

Step 6: Cut the 6" × 24" strips into 6" squares. You will need 4 squares for Side A and 4 squares for Side B.

Sew one square to each end of a 6" × 36" border strip. Be sure to sew a Side A square to a Side A border strip.

Step 7: Add the border strips and squares to the sides of the quilt. Add the A's to Side A; the B's to Side B and a 6" strip of quilt batting underneath the B.

Pin the strips in place. Check to make sure that the seam lines at the squares line up with the seam lines of the first border you added.

Sew at ¼". Open up the border strips. Pin in place. Zigzag the open edges.

Step 8: Add a binding following the directions in the chapter on finishing quilts.

REACHING FINGERS

Finished size: 72" × 83" (double bed)

Fabric needed:
- 8 yards of dark fabric
- 8 yards of light fabric
- ⅔ yard for center color
- ¾ yard for binding
- Fatt Batt™

SIDE A

SIDE B

This design is made up of 4 log cabin quilt blocks which start with a rectangle for the center.

On two sides of the rectangle center, there will be wide strips; the other two sides will have narrow strips. This is what gives an off-centered look to each of the four quilt blocks.

The wide strips on Side A of the quilt are made out of dark fabric; the wide strips on Side B are light colored fabric. The narrow strips are just the opposite — light on Side A; dark on Side B.

Different fabrics may be used for each of the positions. Or the same fabric may be used for all of the dark strips and the same fabric for all of the light strips.

CAUTION: The first time you make this quilt, stick with just one dark and one light fabric. It would be very easy to get confused with a lot of different fabrics.

If you use just one dark and one light fabric for this quilt, you will need 8 yards of each color.

To use different colors throughout the quilt, use the following chart to determine the amount of fabric needed for each position.

FABRIC REQUIREMENTS

Position #		Buy	Cut
1 (center)	Side A	⅓ yard	2 strips 6" × 45"
	Side B	⅓ yard	2 strips 6" × 45"
2 & 3	Side A	½ yard	3 strips dark fabric 6" × 45"
	Side B	½ yard	3 strips light fabric 6" × 45"
4 & 5	Side A	⅓ yard	4 strips light fabric 3" × 45"
	Side B	⅓ yard	4 strips dark fabric 3" × 45"
6 & 7	Side A	¾ yard	4 strips dark fabric 6" × 45"
	Side B	¾ yard	4 strips light fabric 6" × 45"
8 & 9	Side A	½ yard	6 strips light fabric 3" × 45"
	Side B	½ yard	6 strips dark fabric 3" × 45"
10 & 11	Side A	1⅓ yards	8 strips dark fabric 6" × 45"
	Side B	1⅓ yards	8 strips light fabric 6" × 45"
12 & 13	Side A	¾ yard	8 strips light fabric 3" × 45"
	Side B	¾ yard	8 strips dark fabric 3" × 45"
14 & 15	Side A	1⅓ yards	8 strips dark fabric 6" × 45"
	Side B	1⅓ yards	8 strips light fabric 6" × 45"
16 & 17	Side A	¾ yard	8 strips light fabric 3" × 45"
	Side B	¾ yard	8 strips dark fabric 3" × 45"
Fatt Batt™			cut lengthwise in 3" and 6" strips

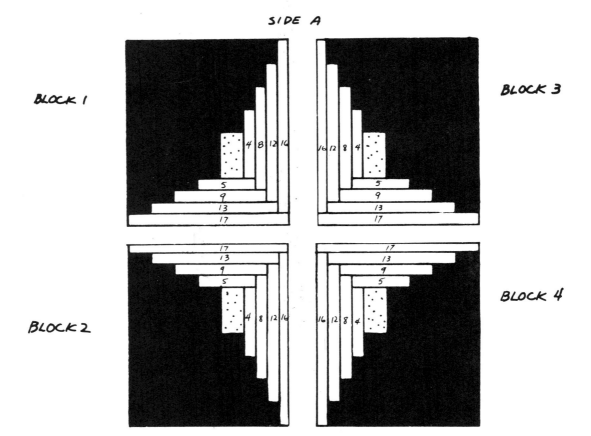

If you use many different colors, make a chart showing the colors you will use in each position. Write in the name of the color or cut a fabric swatch and glue it on the chart.

Side A	Position #	Side B
_____	1 (center)	_____
_____	2 & 3	_____
_____	4 & 5	_____
_____	6 & 7	_____
_____	8 & 9	_____
_____	10 & 11	_____
_____	12 & 13	_____
_____	14 & 15	_____
_____	16 & 17	_____

Step 1: For the centers of all four blocks, cut two strips of the center fabric (position #1, Side A) and two strips of the center fabric for Side B. These strips should be cut 6" x 45".

Cut a 6" wide strip lengthwise from the quilt batting.

On the right side of one A strip, mark a line at ½" and every 12 inches. On the second A strip, mark a line at ½" and mark just one 12 inch section.

You will need four 12 inch sections marked on the position #1 A strip.

(The ½" marked cutting line at the beginning of the strips insures a straight edge and removes the selvage edge from the fabric.)

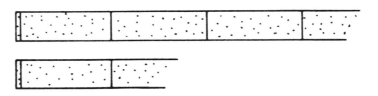

Step 2: Place a 6" strip of quilt batting against the wrong side of the marked strip of fabric (the A strip).

Lay the B strip of fabric with the wrong side against the other side of the quilt batt.

You now have a quilt sandwich — quilt batt with A strip on top and B strip underneath.

Pin along both long edges. Keep the edges of all three pieces even. Stitch close to the edge (less than ¼"). Use a medium width zigzag stitch and a medium stitch length.

CAUTION: Check to see that the edges of fabric are securely caught in the stitching on both sides. After adding the next positions, you will be unable to go back and repair places where the fabric does not catch in the seam.

Pin on both sides of each vertical line.

Stitch at about ⅛" (less than the width of the presser foot) with a medium wide zigzag on each side of the six vertical lines.

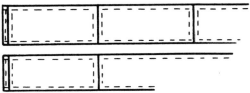

(stitching lines are indicated by broken lines)

Cut into four sections along the marked lines.
You will be cutting in between two rows of stitching.

Step 3: Take a wide light colored strip from position #2, Side B.
Place it right side against one long edge of a finished center piece (position #1).

Place a 6" wide strip of quilt batting underneath the Side B strip.

Place a wide dark fabric strip (position #2, Side A), right side down on the finished center piece (position #1).

From bottom up: quilt batting; wide light colored strip B;
finished center rectangle; wide dark colored strip A.

Pin together carefully keeping all edges even. Use lots of pins to keep it from slipping.

Butt the finished center rectangles next to each other between the wide strips of position #2.

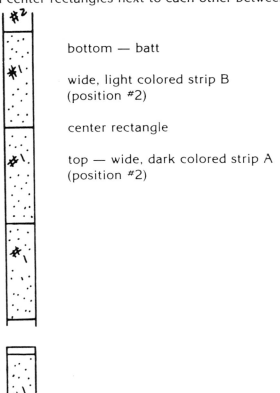

bottom — batt

wide, light colored strip B
(position #2)

center rectangle

top — wide, dark colored strip A
(position #2)

Stitch together at ¼" (use edge of presser foot to keep the seam allowance even).

CUT THE BUTT! Cut each section apart in between sections #1.

CAUTION: Check on both sides to make sure there are no puckers and that all edges are securely caught in the seam.

Only three center sections will fit on one set of strips. The fourth section will have to go between another set of strips.

Trim quilt batt from seam allowance.

Open out position #2 (both fabrics and quilt batt).

Pin all three open edges together carefully. Make sure all fabric and batt edges are even.

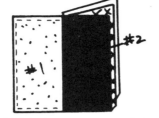

Sew the long edges together first with a wide zigzag stitch.

Sew the short edges together from the outside edge of position #2 toward the seam line between #2 and #1. Use a wide zigzag stitch close to the edge of the fabric.

Side A strips will always be on the top when sewing; Side B will be underneath.

Step 4: *CAUTION:* Put two of the finished #1 and #2 sections aside until Step 12.

Take a wide light colored strip, position #3, Side B. Place it right side up against the short edges of a finished #1 and #2 section.

Place a 6" wide strip of quilt batt against the wrong side of the light colored strip.

Place a wide dark colored strip (position #3, Side A), right side down, on top of the short edges of the finished #1 and #2 section.

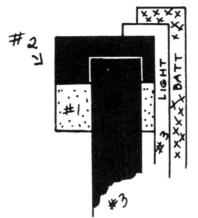

From bottom up — quilt batt, wide light colored strip (Side B), finished #1 and #2 sections, wide dark colored strip (Side A).

Pin together carefully keeping all edges even.

Use lots of pins to keep it from slipping.

CAUTION: Position #2 (Side A) must be at the top of the strips. Always keep the dark #2 up. Remember, the light colored #2 (Side B) should be underneath and next to the light colored strip #3.

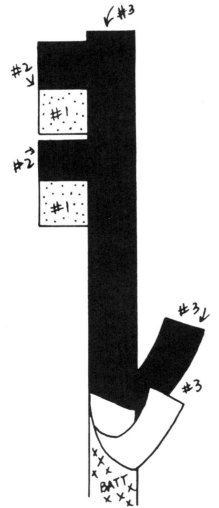

Butt another finished #1 and #2 section up against the first one between the strips.

Stitch at ¼" (width of the presser foot).

CUT THE BUTT! Cut each section apart in between the finished sections #1 and #2.

Trim quilt batt from seam allowance.

Open out position #3 (both fabrics and batt).

Pin all three open edges together carefully.
Make sure all fabric and batt edges are even.

Sew the long edges together. Sew close to the edge with a wide zigzag.

Sew the short edges from the outside edge of position #3 to the seam line between #1, #2, and #3. Use a wide zigzag stitch.

Step 5: Take a narrow dark colored strip (position #4, B). Place it right side against the bottom of a finished #1, #2, and #3B section.

(The bottom section, Side B, has wide light colored strips and narrow dark colored strips.)

Place a 3" strip of quilt batt under the wrong side of the narrow dark strip.

Take a narrow light colored strip (position #4A). Place it right side down against the finished #1, #2, and #3A section.

Pin carefully.
Keep all edges even.

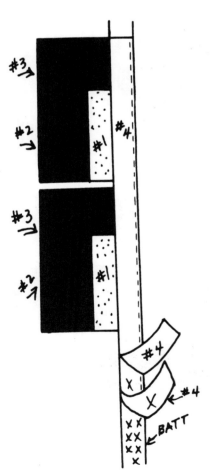

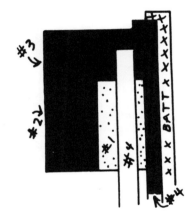

Butt the two finished sections next to each other between the strips.

Position #3 must be at the top of the strips.
Always keep the dark #3A on top.

Stitch at ¼" (width of the presser foot).

CUT THE BUTT!

Trim quilt batt from seam allowance.

— 19 —

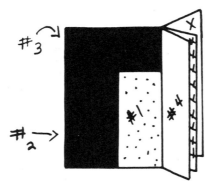

Open out position #4 (both fabrics and the batt).

Pin all three open edges together carefully.
Make sure all fabric and batt edges are even.

Sew the long edges together with a wide zigzag stitch. Sew the short edges together from the outside edge toward position #1. Sew close to the outside edge.

Step 6: Take a narrow dark colored strip (position #5B).
Place it right side toward the bottom of the finished #1, #2, #3, and #4B.

(The bottom section, Side B, has wide light colored strips and narrow dark colored strips.)

Place a 3" strip of quilt batt under the wrong side of the dark colored strip.

Take a narrow light colored strip (position #5A).
Place it right side down against the finished #1, #2, #3, and #4A section.

Pin carefully.
Keep all edges even.

The position #4 narrow light colored strip should be at the top of the strips.

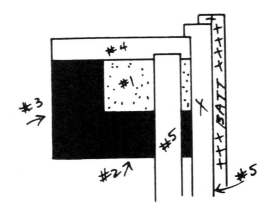

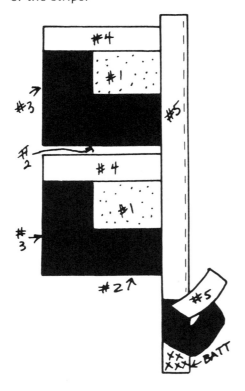

Stitch at ¼".
CUT THE BUTT! Cut #5 strips apart between the sections.
Trim quilt batt from seam allowance.
Open out position #5 (two strips of fabric and a strip of batt).

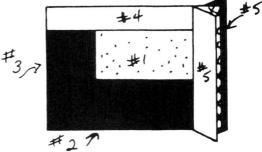

CAUTION: Make sure there are no puckers on the top or bottom of the quilt squares.

— 20 —

Pin all three open edges together carefully.

Sew the long edges of position #5 together close to the edge with a wide zigzag stitch.

Sew the short edges from the outside edge of position #5 in toward the seam line between #1, #2, #4, and #5.

Step 7: Position #6A will have a wide dark colored strip on the top and a wide light colored (B) strip on the bottom.

Always place the last strip you have added at the top when sewing the next strip on to the quilt block. At this step position #5 will be at the top with the light colored strip (A) on the top.

As the strips get longer, it will be easier to just work with one block at a time instead of butting them along the strip of fabric.

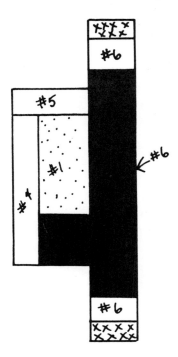

From bottom up:
    6" strip of quilt batt on bottom
    wide light colored strip (6B) right side up
    quilt block with #5 light colored strip at the top
    wide dark colored strip (6A), right side down

Pin all edges together carefully.

Stitch at ¼" from long outside edge.

Trim the strips and quilt batt even with the edges of the quilt block.

Trim quilt batt from seam allowance.

Open out position #6.
Make sure there are no puckers.

Pin all three edges (wide dark strip, wide light strip, quilt batt).

Sew the long edges together first.
Use a wide zigzag, medium length stitch.
Sew close to the edge.

Sew the short edges with a wide zigzag stitch.

Step 8: Add the strips in position #7.

Position #6 should be at the top of the strips with the wide dark strip (A) showing; the wide light strip (B) will be underneath.

From bottom up:
    6" strip of quilt batt on bottom
    wide light colored strip (7B), right side up
    quilt block with #6 dark colored strip at top
    wide dark colored strip (7A), right side down

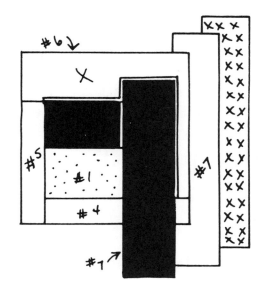

Pin the edges together.
Stitch at ¼".
Trim the ends of the strips and quilt batt.
Trim the quilt batt from the seam allowance.
Open out position #7. Pin all three edges together.
Sew the edges with a wide zigzag close to the outside edge.

Step 9: Add the strips in position #8 in this order:

> 3" wide strip of quilt batting on bottom
> dark narrow strip #8B right side up
> quilt block with #7A dark colored strip at the top
> light narrow strip #8A right side down

Pin the edges together; stitch at ¼".

Trim the ends of the strips and the batt.

Trim the quilt batt from the seam allowance.

Open out position #8; pin all three edges together.
Zigzag the open edges.

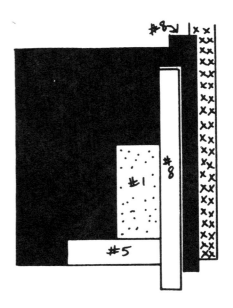

Step 10: Add the strips in position #9:

> 3" wide strip of quilt batting
> dark narrow strip #9B right side up
> quilt block with #8A light colored strip at the top
> light narrow strip #9A right side down

Pin and stitch.

Trim the ends of the strips; trim the quilt batting
from the seam allowance. Open out #9 strips.
Pin the edges; zigzag.

Step 11: Continue adding strips until all 17 positions are finished.

Remember:

> The last strip added always goes at the top when adding the next strip.
>
> The narrow light colored strips are always facing you; the narrow dark colored strips are underneath.
>
> The wide dark colored strips are always facing you; the wide light colored strips are underneath.

On the 16th and 17th positions, do not zigzag the edges together.
They need to have their edges loose to sew the blocks together.

Step 12: Take the two other finished #1 and #2 sections from Step 4.

These two blocks will have the positions added in the opposite direction. This is necessary if you want to have the four quilt squares form a dark cross in the center on Side B and a light cross in the center on Side A.

> *CAUTION:* When adding another strip, the last strip added will be at the bottom. This is opposite to the directions up to Step 11.
>
> The A Side will still be facing up; the B Side will be underneath.

Add the strips in position #3:

> 6" side strip of quilt batt
> wide light colored strip 3B right side up
> Position #1 and #2 with wide dark strip at the bottom
> Wide dark strip 3A right side down

Pin and stitch at ¼".

Trim quilt batt from the seam allowance.

Open out position #3.

Pin all three edges together; zigzag with widest stitch.

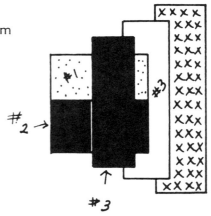

— 22 —

Step 13: Add the strips in position #4:

> 3" wide strip of quilt batt
> narrow dark colored strip 4B right side up
> quilt block with #3 strip at bottom
> narrow light colored strip 4A right side down

Pin and stitch at ¼".

Trim quilt batt from the seam allowance.

Open out position #4.

Pin all edges together; zigzag edges.

Step 14: Add the strips in position #5:

> 3" wide strip of quilt batt
> narrow dark colored strip 5B right side up
> quilt block with #4 (narrow light strip) at the bottom
> narrow light colored strip 5A right side down

Pin and stitch at ¼".

Trim quilt batt from the seam allowance.

Open out position #5; pin all edges together; zigzag.

Your quilt block will now look like this:

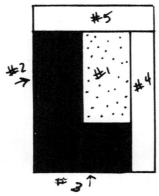

Step 15: Continue adding strips until all 17 positions are finished.

> *REMEMBER:* Just for these two log cabin blocks, the last strip added always goes at the **bottom** when adding the next strip.
>
> *REMEMBER:* The narrow light colored strips (A) are always up; the narrow dark colored strips are down (B).
>
> *REMEMBER:* The wide dark colored strips (A) are always up; the wide light strips (B) are down.
>
> *CAUTION:* On the 16th and 17th positions, do not zigzag the edges together. They need to be loose to sew the blocks together.

ASSEMBLING THE BLOCKS (Method 1)

Step 1: Place the four completed blocks into the desired pattern.

> Sew two blocks together by placing Side A's together (wide dark strips and narrow light strips).
>
> Pin just the narrow light strips; sew with ¼" seam.
>
> Lay the two blocks right side down; butt the quilt batt strips next to each other. Trim the batt if it overlaps. Whip stitch by hand the quilt batt together.
>
> One seam allowance (narrow dark strip) will lay flat. The other seam allowance should be turned under ¼" and pinned on top of the flat seam allowance.
>
> Blind stitch by hand.
>
> Sew the other two blocks together.

Step 2: Sew the center seam together — right sides together.
Finish the back seam allowance the same way as in Step 1.
You now have a reversible quilt/comforter.

ASSEMBLING THE BLOCKS (Method 2) — Enclosed Seam Allowance

Step 1: Zigzag the edges together on the strips in the 16th and 17th positions on all four blocks.

Step 2: Cut four strips of dark fabric 1½" × 45".

Step 3: Place the four completed blocks in the desired pattern with Side A facing up.

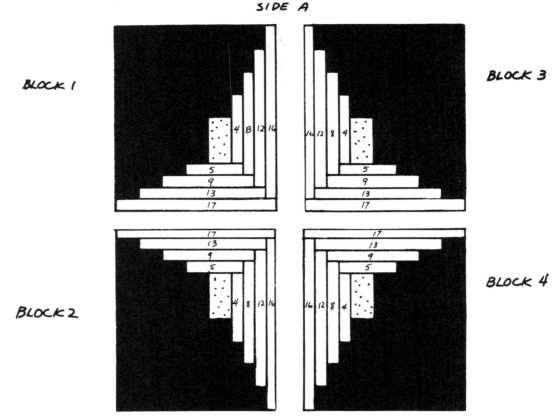

Step 4: Pin blocks 1 and 2 together with Sides A together.
CAUTION: Open up the blocks. Check to see that the vertical seams line up even though the seam lines do not come together.
Pin the narrow 1½" dark strip right side down against the two blocks. Keep the edge of the strip even with the edges of the blocks.
Sew at ¼" through all layers.
Trim the quilt batt from the seam allowance.
Sew blocks 3 and 4 together in the same way, including the 1½" wide strip.

Step 5: Enclose the seam allowance by bringing the 1½" strip of fabric over the seam allowance.
Fold under ¼" on the unsewn edge of the strip and pin the folded edge to the seam allowance. (Do not pin to the quilt blocks — only to the seam allowance.)
Topstitch by machine through the 1½" strip and the seam allowance OR blindstitch by hand.
The covered seam allowance will stand up from the quilt blocks and will add a design feature.

Step 6:   Sew two of the 1½" strips together lengthwise.
This will give you a strip 1½" x 85/88".

Pin blocks 1 and 2 to blocks 3 and 4.

Pin the 1½" strip, right sides down, with the edge of the strip even with the edges of the blocks.

Make sure the seam line between the two sewn-together strips is directly in the middle of the seam (where the two blocks are joined together).

Sew through all layers with ¼" seam allowance.

Trim the quilt batt from the center where four seams come together.

Step 7:   Enclose the seam allowance by bringing the 1½" strip of fabric over the seam allowance.

Fold under ¼" on the unsewn edge of the strip and pin the folded edge to the seam allowance.

Topstitch by machine or blindstitch by hand.

This seam allowance will also stand up from the quilt blocks to give a three-dimensional effect to the one side of your quilt.

Step 8:   Bind the edges of your quilt/comforter with straight or bias cut binding.

VARIATIONS:

- Try cutting the 1½" strips from light colored fabric or from a completely different fabric from that used in the quilt blocks.
- The binding could repeat the color used in the center of the blocks; it could be a darker color to serve as a frame for the quilt; or it could be one of the colors from a print used in the quilt.
- Make the center an interesting print. If quilting on the print is desirable, do it after the center is finished, but before the strips are added. If the print has a top and bottom, be careful in what direction the print is placed.
- Patchwork quilt block for the center can be quilted to just a piece of batting before making the quilt sandwich for the center.
- Stencil a design in the center; the stencilled design can be carried out on some or all of the strips forming the quilt. Try a cat sitting in the center block as though it was a window; leaves from a tree can be stencilled on the strips; why not a stencilled mouse under the window sill.
- Try a reversible applique design. The directions for this technique are in the section on reversible applique.
- For a wall hanging or a tablecloth, decrease the width of the strips: 3" and 1½" wide strips will give you a finished size of 36" x 41" (the center should be 3" x 6"). Use a light weight quilt batting or fleece for a reversible tablecloth.
- Use strips cut 1" and 2" (center 2" x 4") to get a finished piece that measures 24" x 28".

KAYE'S WASTE BASKET QUILT

I started making this type of quilt when I was teaching several six-week quilting classes. The last night of the class, I would take a finished quilt top to class that was made out of the scraps my students had thrown away during the six weeks. Then each student had to sign at least one of the fabrics that had been hers.

If you are going to scrounge in the wastebasket after class, I would suggest emptying it before class. It is much easier to just have fabric to remove. If you really plan ahead, which I usually do not do, you could put plastic bags in the wastebasket right before class. Then just take the plastic bags out at the end of class. Do not encourage eating and drinking in class if you are going to raid the wastebaskets.

Also, if you let your students in on what you are doing, the pickings in the wastebasket get very slim.

These quilts are great to take to the beach or on a hayride; my teenagers preferred these to any of the other quilts I made.

Denim from outgrown or worn-out jeans looks great. All of the shades of blue blend together into a comfortable looking quilt.

Corduroy cut in different directions looks like many different shades of the same color. Try using all of those double-knit fabrics that we all have in our fabric collection.

Each side of this reversible quilt can be made of a different fabric.

All the fabrics used should be machine washable. This is the kind of quilt that you will use and wash a lot.

If you are using denim or double-knit for both sides of this quilt, you may not need the quilt batting in between. This quilt will be very warm and heavy without the quilt batting.

To make this quilt:

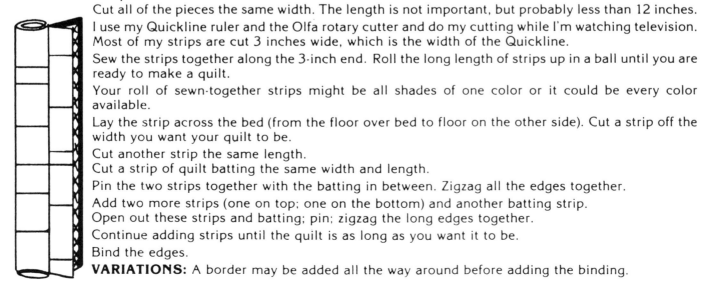

Cut all of the pieces the same width. The length is not important, but probably less than 12 inches.

I use my Quickline ruler and the Olfa rotary cutter and do my cutting while I'm watching television. Most of my strips are cut 3 inches wide, which is the width of the Quickline.

Sew the strips together along the 3-inch end. Roll the long length of strips up in a ball until you are ready to make a quilt.

Your roll of sewn-together strips might be all shades of one color or it could be every color available.

Lay the strip across the bed (from the floor over bed to floor on the other side). Cut a strip off the width you want your quilt to be.

Cut another strip the same length.

Cut a strip of quilt batting the same width and length.

Pin the two strips together with the batting in between. Zigzag all the edges together.

Add two more strips (one on top; one on the bottom) and another batting strip.

Open out these strips and batting; pin; zigzag the long edges together.

Continue adding strips until the quilt is as long as you want it to be.

Bind the edges.

VARIATIONS: A border may be added all the way around before adding the binding.

BARN RAISING

Finished size: 75" × 75" (Double Bed)

Fabric needed: 8 yards for each side

Binding: ¾ yard

1 Fatt Batt™

My quilt is done in various shades of rose on one side; dusty blues on the reverse side. The rose colors start with the darkest shade in the center; the blues start with the lightest shade in the center.

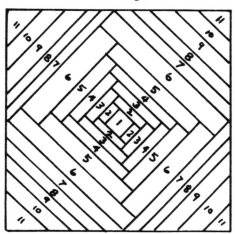

FABRIC REQUIREMENTS

Position #		Buy	Cut
1 (center)	Side A	¼ yard	8" × 8"
	Side B	¼ yard	8" × 8"
	Batting		8" × 8"
2	Side A	⅛ yard	1 strip 4" × 45"
	Side B	⅛ yard	1 strip 4" × 45"
3	Side A	⅓ yard	2 strips 5" × 45"
	Side B	⅓ yard	2 strips 5" × 45"
4	Side A	¾ yard	4 strips 6" × 45"
	Side B	¾ yard	4 strips 6" × 45"
5	Side A	1 yard	4 strips 7" × 45"
	Side B	1 yard	4 strips 7" × 45"
6	Side A	1½ yards	6 strips 8" × 45"
	Side B	1½ yards	6 strips 8" × 45"
7	Side A	¾ yard	8 strips 3" × 45"
	Side B	¾ yard	8 strips 3" × 45"
8	Side A	1 yard	8 strips 4" × 45"
	Side B	1 yard	8 strips 4" × 45"
9	Side A	1¼ yards	8 strips 5" × 45"
	Side B	1¼ yards	8 strips 5" × 45"
10	Side A	¾ yard	4 strips 6" × 45"
	Side B	¾ yard	4 strips 6" × 45"
11	Side A	½ yard	2 strips 7" × 45"
	Side B	½ yard	2 strips 7" × 45"
	Fatt Batt™		(cut lengthwise) as needed
	Binding	¾ yard	7 strips 3" × 45"

Step 1: Make a chart of the colors you will use in each position. This will help in planning both sides of your quilt and will keep the strips of color in order.

Cut fabric swatches (or write a description of the fabric); glue or tape them in place opposite the "position #" column under "Side A" and "Side B."

This is the chart I made for my Rose/Blue quilt:

Side A	Position #	Side B
dark rose/pink flowers	1 (center)	beige/lt. blue flowers
dark rose/large lt. rose flowers	2	lt. blue/white stripes
rose/white flowers	3	lt. blue/small white flowers
rose/white flowers & leaves	4	lt. blue/white leaves
pink flowers	5	dk. blue pin dot
beige/lt. rose flowers	6	dk. blue/large lt. blue flowers
dark rose/pink flowers	7	lt. blue/white stripes
rose/white flowers	8	lt. blue/small white flowers
rose/white flowers & leaves	9	lt. blue/white leaves
beige/lt. rose flowers	10	dk. blue pin dot
dark rose/large lt. rose flowers	11	dk. blue/large lt. blue flowers

Positions #1 thru #6 were the six colors used in my quilt. Positions #7 thru #11 used some of those six colors again.

My binding was cut from the darkest rose color for two reasons: I like a dark binding (it frames the quilt nicely) and it was the only one of the fabrics in the quilt which had both rose and blue in the print.

Step 2: Cut an 8" × 8" square for the center from both Side A and Side B fabrics listed for position #1 (center).

Cut an 8" × 8" square of Fatt Batt™.

Make a quilt sandwich: pin three layers together — Side B square right side down; Fatt Batt™; Side A fabric right side up.

Zigzag around all four sides.

CAUTION: If one fabric is very dark and the other is very light, the dark fabric may show through the light fabric. If it does, place two layers of light fabric together OR place one layer of light fabric under the dark fabric.

SIDE B WILL ALWAYS BE ON THE BOTTOM AS NEW STRIPS ARE ADDED.

Step 3: Take the 4" wide strips from position #2 on the chart.

Place the B strip right side against the Side B center square.

Place the A strip right side against Side A of the center square.

Place a 4" strip of Fatt Batt™ under the B Strip.

Pin all four layers together (Fatt Batt™; B Strip; center square; A strip).

Sew using ¼" seam allowance along the length of the center square

Trim the edges of the strips and batting even with the center square.

Trim quilt batt from the seam allowance.

Open out position #2 (both fabrics and quilt batt).

Pin all three open edges together carefully.

Zigzag the open edges.

Step 4: Sew the 4" wide strips from position #2 to the opposite side of the center square. Follow the directions in Step 3.

Sew the 4" strips from position #2 to the two remaining sides of the center square.

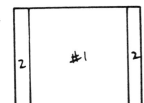

Step 5: Add the strips cut from both A and B Sides of position #3, #4, #5 and #6 by following the same directions.

REMEMBER:
B strips are always on the bottom.
quilt batt is placed under the B strip.

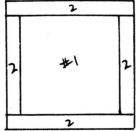

always start a new position by adding strips to the same two sides of the square.

CAUTION: If the strips are not long enough, they should be pieced in the center of the length (this should only be necessary in position #6).

Step 6: After adding the strips from position #7, open out the strips; pin the edges together; zigzag the open edges.

THEN the ends of the strips should be trimmed using the Starmaker⑧ quilting tool.

Line up the long edge of the Starmaker⑧ along the seam line.

Trim along the ⑧ angle.

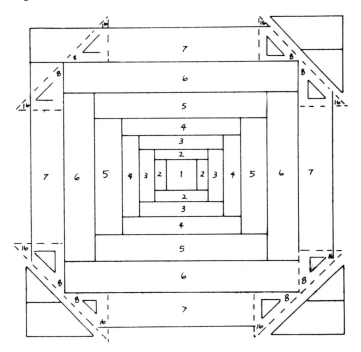

Step 7: Continue adding the rest of the strips.
Trim the ends of each strip by using the Starmaker⑧.

Step 8: Apply the binding as shown in the chapter on finishing reversible quilts.

VARIATIONS:
- To make this quilt larger, add more strips between position #6 and #7.
- Top and bottom borders may also be added to make this quilt rectangular.
- Or start with a diamond shape in the center instead of a square. Directions for a diamond-shaped center are on the following pages.
- Use a Reverse Silhouette Applique in the center block. See Chapter III.

CHAPTER II

KING OF DIAMONDS

Finished size: 67" x 115"

Fabric needed: 10 yards each side

Binding: 1 yard

Fatt Batt™: King Size — cut lengthwise in 8" strips

This diamond-shaped quilt is very pretty, and with the right tool, the Starmaker⑥, it becomes a very easy quilt. The Starmaker tools were designed to make those patchwork patterns with angles become just as easy to mark, cut and sew as patterns using squares and rectangles.

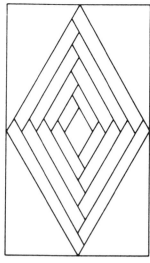

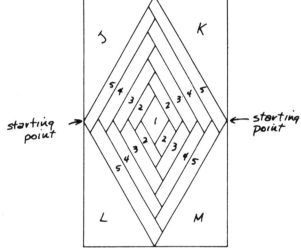

FABRIC REQUIREMENTS

Position #		Buy	Cut
1 (center)	Side A	½ yard	diamond with 8" sides
	Side B	½ yard	diamond with 8" sides
	Batting		diamond with 8" sides
2	Side A	½ yard	2 strips 8" x 45"
	Side B	½ yard	2 strips 8" x 45"
3	Side A	½ yard	2 strips 8" x 45"
	Side B	½ yard	2 strips 8" x 45"
4	Side A	1 yard	4 strips 8" x 45"
	Side B	1 yard	4 strips 8" x 45"
5	Side A	2 yards	8 strips 8" x 45"
	Side B	2 yards	8 strips 8" x 45"
	Fatt Batt		cut lengthwise in 8" strips
	Binding	1 yard	9 strips 3" x 45"
JKLM	Side A	3½ yards	2 pieces 41" x 60"
	Side B	3½ yards	2 pieces 41" x 60"
	Batting		2 pieces 41" x 60"

A border added on each side (8" wide) will give a finished quilt of approximately 80" x 115".

Step 1: Make a chart of the colors or fabrics you have chosen for this diamond quilt.

Side A	Position #	Side B
_____	1 (center)	_____
_____	2	_____
_____	3	_____
_____	4	_____
_____	5	_____
_____	JKLM	_____

Step 2: Mark the diamond shape on the center fabric. Use the Starmaker⑥. Each side of the diamond should be 8 inches long.

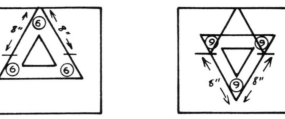

Cut out a diamond for Side A and Side B.
Cut a piece of quilt batting the same shape.
Pin all three layers together: Side B right side down; quilt batting; Side A right side up.
Zigzag all the edges.
SIDE B WILL ALWAYS BE ON THE BOTTOM AS NEW STRIPS ARE ADDED.

Step 3: Take the strips from position #2.

Place the B strip right side up against one side of the B center diamond.
Place a strip of quilt batting against the wrong side of the B strip.

Place the A strip right side down against the A center diamond.

Pin all layers together. Sew with ¼" seam allowance.

Trim the quilt batt from the seam allowance.

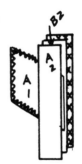

Open out position #2. Pin carefully.
Lay the Starmaker⑥ tool on the diamond center and the strip as shown.

On one end of the #2 strip, the Starmaker⑥ will lay on the outside of piece #1. Mark that angle on the strip.

At the other end of the #2 strip, the Starmaker will be placed on the inside of piece #1 and #2 to mark the angle.

Cut on these marked lines.

Zigzag all the open edges.

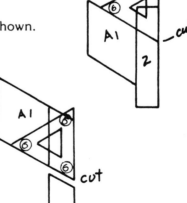

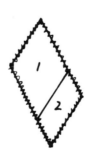

— 31 —

Step 4: Add #2 strips to the second side of the center diamond.

Place the Side B strip right side against the B diamond; the Side A strip right side against the A diamond; a strip of quilt batting underneath the B strip.

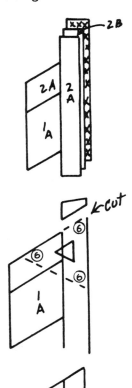

Pin all layers together carefully.

Sew with ¼" seam allowance.

Trim the quilt batt from the seam allowance.

Open out these position #2 strips.

Pin the edges together carefully.

Using the Starmaker⑥, mark the angles on the ends of these strips.

Cut the ends of the strips.

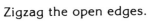

Zigzag the open edges.

CAUTION: After adding each strip, check both Side A and Side B to make sure the fabric is caught in the seam allowance.

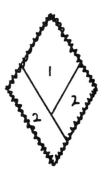

Step 5: Add #2 strips to the third side of the diamond center.

Place the Side B strip right side against the B diamond; Side A strip right side against the A diamond; strip of quilt batting underneath B strip.

Pin the edges together carefully.

Sew with ¼" seam allowance.

Trim quilt batting from the seam allowance.

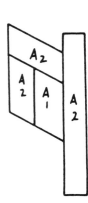

Open out these position #2 strips.
Pin the edges together carefully.

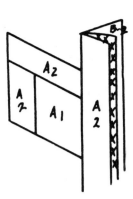

Using the Starmaker⑥, mark the angles on the ends of these strips. Cut the ends.

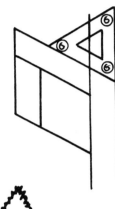

Zigzag the open edges.

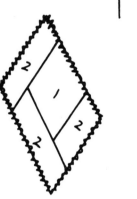

Step 6: Add #2 strips to the fourth side of the diamond center.

Place the Side B strip right side against the B diamond; Side A strip right side against the A diamond; strip of quilt batting underneath the B strip.

Pin the edges together carefully.

Sew with ¼" seam allowance.

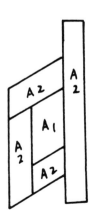

Open out these position #2 strips.
Pin the edges together carefully.
NOTICE THAT WHEN ADDING STRIPS TO THE CENTER DIAMOND, THE LAST PIECE THAT WAS ADDED TO THE CENTER IS ALWAYS AT THE TOP OF THE STRIP. (In this case, the third side was the last one added so that piece lays at the top when adding the fourth side.

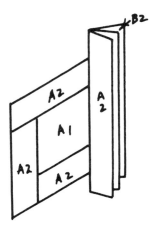
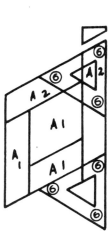

Using the Starmaker⑥, mark and cut both ends of this new strip.
Zigzag the open edges.

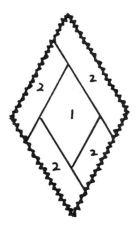

Step 7: Continue adding strips from position #3, #4, and #5.

Always keep the last piece that was added at the top (or, in other words, at the beginning of the stitching) when adding the next strip.

Always use the Starmaker⑥ to accurately cut the angles.

Step 8: To cut the pieces for JKLM:
Cut two pieces of Side A fabric 41" × 60".
Cut two pieces of Side B fabric 41" × 60".

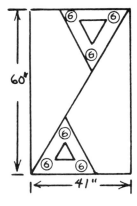

Mark one Side A piece and one Side B piece on the wrong side of the fabric by using the Starmaker⑥ at the top and bottom to get the correct angle for the diagonal cutting line.

Place the two Side A fabrics right sides together with the marked fabric on top.

Pin together.

Cut on the diagonal line.

This will give you the four corners for Side A.

Place the two Side B fabrics right sides together with the marked fabric on top.

Pin together. Cut on the diagonal line.

This will give you the four corners for Side B.

Cut two pieces of quilt batt 41" × 60". Cut these diagonally using Starmaker⑥.

(I have allowed enough material for these corner pieces to take into account slight differences in seam allowances.)

Step 9: Starting at the narrow angle of the corner pieces and the wide angle at the side of the center diamond, pin Side A corner pieces to Side A of the diamond, right sides together. Pin Side B corner pieces to Side B of the diamond, right sides together. Pin the quilt batting piece under Side B.

Open out the corner pieces; pin all layers together.

Zigzag the open edges.

Sew with ¼" seam allowances.

(You may have to trim the top, bottom and sides of the corner pieces even with the tips of the diamond.)

Step 10: Apply the binding. See the chapter on finishing techniques.

VARIATIONS:

- The corners of this quilt can be made from a large floral pattern on Side A and a solid colored fabric on Side B. Quilting could be done around the floral print. Just the quilting would show on Side B.

- The corners could be stencilled. The stencilling should be done before the corners are sewn to the diamond. Both sides could be stencilled — the quilting would be done parallel to the lines of the diamond. OR the corners could be tied in a design to compliment the stencilling.

  If only one side of the quilt is stencilled, quilting could be done to accent the stencilling. Only the quilting would show on the other side of the quilt.

- The corners could be quilted in rows parallel to the diamond shape. Use the Starmaker⑥ to mark the quilting lines.

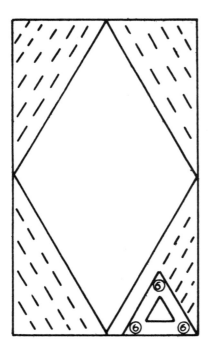 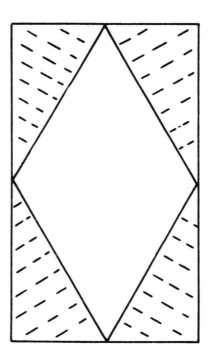

- The corners could also be quilted at right angles to the diamond shape.

STARMAKER WALL HANGING

Finished size: 21" x 31"
(Type of fabric used; type of quilt batting; and width of seam allowance all affect the finished size.)

Batting: Fatt Batt™ 21" x 31"

This diamond patterned wall hanging is easy to make accurately with the Starmaker⑥ quilting tool.

Try one side in all neutral colors; the other in shiny or bright fabrics.

Try this in velvets or ultrasuede for different room decors.

The directions call for a different fabric to be used for each strip added, like a scrap quilt. If you prefer the look of diamonds within diamonds, assemble the diamond shape according to the directions for the King Size Diamond Quilt.

Each additional set of 4 strips around the center diamond will add 3½" to the width and approximately 5½" to the height.

Try this wall hanging with Fatt Batt™ used in the diamond; then use a light weight batting for the vertical strips. This will give you a difference in texture that can be quite interesting.

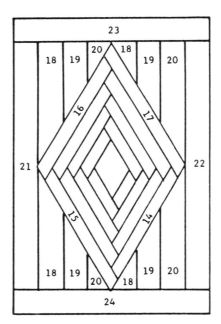

This pattern also makes a beautiful tablecloth; but use a light weight quilt batting.

— 36 —

FABRIC REQUIREMENTS

Position #		Cut
1 (center)	Side A	diamond with 4" sides
	Side B	diamond with 4" sides
	Batting	diamond with 4" sides
2	Side A	1 strip 2" × 6"
	Side B	1 strip 2" × 6"
3	Side A	1 strip 2" × 9"
	Side B	1 strip 2" × 9"
4	Side A	1 strip 2" × 9"
	Side B	1 strip 2" × 9"
5	Side A	1 strip 2" × 11"
	Side B	1 strip 2" × 11"
6	Side A	1 strip 2" × 11"
	Side B	1 strip 2" × 11"
7	Side A	1 strip 2" × 14"
	Side B	1 strip 2" × 14"
8	Side A	1 strip 2" × 14"
	Side B	1 strip 2" × 14"
9	Side A	1 strip 2" × 16"
	Side B	1 strip 2" × 16"
10	Side A	1 strip 2" × 16"
	Side B	1 strip 2" × 16"
11	Side A	1 strip 2" × 20"
	Side B	1 strip 2" × 20"
12	Side A	1 strip 2" × 20"
	Side B	1 strip 2" × 20"
13	Side A	1 strip 2" × 21"
	Side B	1 strip 2" × 21"
14	Side A	1 strip 2" × 21"
	Side B	1 strip 2" × 21"
15	Side A	1 strip 2" × 25"
	Side B	1 strip 2" × 25"
16	Side A	1 strip 2" × 25"
	Side B	1 strip 2" × 25"
17	Side A	1 strip 2" × 26"
	Side B	1 strip 2" × 26"
18-22	Side A	each position—1 strip 3½" × 27"
	Side B	each position—1 strip 3½" × 27"
23 & 24	Side A	each position—1 strip 3½" × 30"
	Side B	each position—1 strip 3½" × 30"
	Batting	cut lengthwise in 2" and 3½" strips
	Binding	4 strips 3" × 45"

Add more borders on the sides to make the wallhanging wider; add more borders on the top and bottom to make the wallhanging higher.

Step 1: Make a chart of the colors you have decided to use:
For a sample chart see the chart for the King Size Diamond quilt.

Step 2: Mark the diamond shape on the center fabrics. Use the Starmaker⑥. Each side of the diamond should be 4" long.

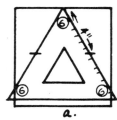 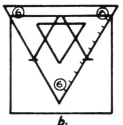 

a.   b.

       a. Lay the Starmaker⑥ on the fabric with the ruler edge along the side. Draw a line from the point at the top down 4 inches along that side. Turn the Starmaker over so the ruled edge is along the other side. Draw a line from the point at the top down 4 inches along that side.

       b. Turn the Starmaker upside down to mark the bottom of the diamond. Line the 4" mark on the ruler with the ends of the 4" lines from Step a. Draw both sides from the point to the previous lines.

       c. Your finished diamond.

Cut out a diamond for Side A and Side B.
Cut a piece of quilt batting the same shape.
Pin all three layers together; Side B right side down; quilt batting; Side A right side up.
Zigzag all the edges.
SIDE B WILL ALWAYS BE UNDERNEATH AS NEW STRIPS ARE ADDED.

Step 3: Take the strips from position #2.

Place the B strip right side up against one side of the B center diamond. Place a strip of quilt batting underneath strip B.

Place the A strip right side down against the A diamond.

Pin all layers together. Sew with ¼" seam allowance.

Trim the quilt batt from the seam allowance.

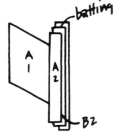

Open out position #2. Pin carefully.

Lay the Starmaker⑥ tool on the diamond center and the strip as shown — on one end of the #2 strip the Starmaker⑥ will lay on the outside of piece #1.
Mark and cut that angle. At the other end of the #2 strip, place the Starmaker on the inside of the center diamond and strip #2. Mark and cut that angle.

Zigzag all the open edges.

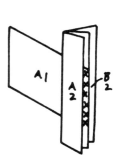

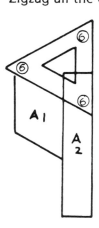 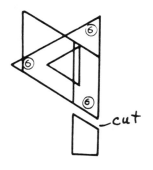 

Step 4: Take the strips from position #3.

Place the B strip right side up against the second side of the B center diamond. Place a 2" strip of quilt batting underneath strip B.

Place the A strip right side down against the A diamond. Pin all layers together. Sew with ¼" seam allowance.

Trim the quilt batt from the seam allowance.

Open out these #3 strips. Pin the edges together carefully.

Use the Starmaker⑥ to mark and cut the ends of the strips.

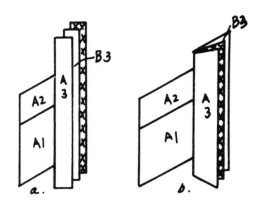

Zigzag the open edges.

CAUTION: The last piece added should always lay toward the top of the new strip, e.g., when adding strip #3, position #2 will be at the top (or away from you as you begin sewing).

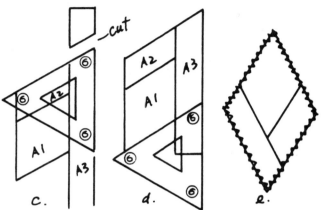

Step 5: Take the strips from position #4.

Place the B strip right side up against the third side of the B center diamond. Place the quilt batting underneath strip B.

The A strip goes right side down against the A diamond.

Pin all the layers together carefully. Sew at ¼".

Trim the quilt batt from the seam allowance.

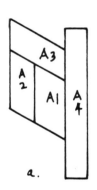

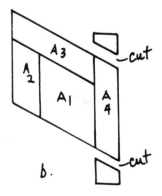

Open out these strips; pin edges together.
Use the Starmaker⑥ to mark and cut the ends of the strips.

Zigzag all the open edges.

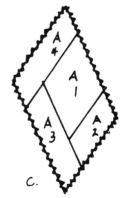

Step 6: Take the strips from position #5.

Place the B strip right side up against the fourth side of the B center diamond. Place the quilt batting underneath strip B.

The A strip goes right side down against the A diamond.

Pin together carefully; sew at ¼".

Trim the quilt batt from the seam allowance.

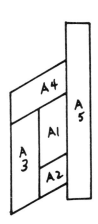

Open out these strips; pin edges together.
Use the Starmaker⑥ to mark and cut the ends of the strips.

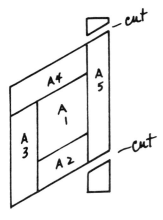

Zigzag all the open edges.

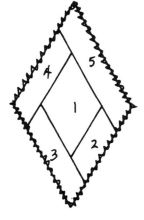

Step 7: Continue adding strips for position 6 thru 17.

Always keep Side B underneath.

The last piece added should always lay toward the top of the new strip.

Use the Starmaker⑥ to insure accurate angles.

Always zigzag the open edges after adding new strips, EXCEPT DO NOT zigzag the edges of strips in position #14, #15, #16, and #17. These must remain open to finish B side after adding the vertical strips.

Step 8: The vertical background strips and the batting are cut 3¼" wide.

Take position #18 strips for both Side A and Side B.

Make a quilt sandwich: Side A strip; batting; Side B strip.

Keep the wrong side of the strips against the batting.

Pin all the edges together carefully; zigzag the edges together.

Check to see that the fabric is caught into the zigzag stitches on both sides of the strip.

Step 9: Add position #19 strips to the #18 quilt sandwich; add #19, Side A to Side A of #18; #19 B strip should be added to Side B of #18. Lay the quilt batt strip underneath the B strip.

Pin the edges together carefully; stitch with ¼" seam allowance.

Trim the quilt batt from the seam allowance.

Open up the #19 strips and quilt batt. Pin together; zigzag the edges. Add strip to #20 to strip #19 in the same way.

Step 10: Draw a horizontal line across the center of this section. Use the Starmaker ⑥ to make diagonal lines. Pin the layers together on each side of every cutting line. Cut between the pins on the marked lines. You will have 4 sections — one for each of the 4 sides of the diamond.

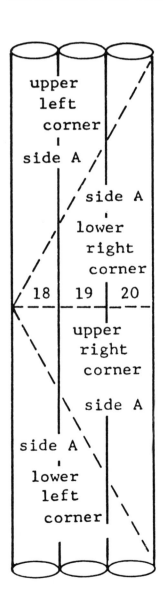

You will need only one of these sections.

— 41 —

Step 11: Place all four pieces in position around the center diamond.

Starting at the narrow angle of the corner pieces and the wide angle at the side of the center diamond, pin Side A corner pieces to Side A of the diamond, right sides together.

CAUTION: Pin the corner pieces to only Side A of the diamond; do not pin through to Side B of the diamond.

Sew with ¼" seam allowance.

Trim the quilt batt from the seam allowance.

Fold under the edge of the strip on the B side of the diamond. Pin the folded edge to the B side of the corner piece. Blind stitch by hand.

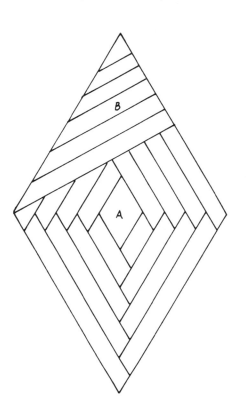

VARIATION: You might prefer to add these four corner pieces by using an enclosed seam allowance on Side B.

To do this, zigzag the edges of the strips in position #14, #15, #16, and #17.

Cut a 1½" wide strip of fabric which will cover the seam allowance. You will need four of these 1½" wide strips. (This strip will outline the diamond shape and will be very predominate in your design — choose your color to give the effect you want.)

Pin the corner pieces to the diamond, starting at the narrow angle of the triangle and the wide angle of the center diamond. Side A of the triangle should be right sides together with Side A of the diamond. Pin through all the pieces of the triangle and all the pieces of the diamond.

Pin the 1½" strip, right side down, so one long edge is even with the pinned edge of the triangle and diamond.

Sew through all layers with ¼" seam allowance.

Fold the other long edge of the 1½" strip under; wrap the strip over the seam allowance; pin the folded edge to the seam line. Stitch through the strip and the seam allowance by machine or blind stitch by hand.

Step 12: Add strips from position #21 and #22. Add both Side A, Side B and quilt batting strips at the same time.

Zigzag the edges closed.

Step 13: Add the top and bottom strips from positions #23 and #24. Add both side A, side B, and quilt batting strips at the same time.

Zigzag the edges of strip #24; zigzag the long edge of #23 — do not zigzag the short side ends of #23. (These will be left open and bound separately so a casing will be formed for hanging this wall hanging.)

Step 14: Bind the top edge of strip #23 first; completely finish this edge before doing any of the rest of the binding. See directions for cutting and applying binding in the chapter on finishing quilts.

Then bind one of the short ends of strip #23. Begin where strip #23 joins strip #22 on Side B. Sew up to the top of strip #23; then attach the binding to the A side of the short end of #23. (*REMEMBER:* this has to be open to form a casing; so do NOT sew through both Side A and Side B.)

Continue down the side of the wall hanging, across the bottom, and up the other side.

Go up Side A of strip #23, go over the top and down the B side of strip #23.

Fold over the binding; blind stitch by hand, or topstitch by machine.

You might want to think of binding this opening for a casing as being the same as binding the armhole on a sleeveless vest. You may want to put this part of the binding on entirely by hand because the opening is so small.

VARIATIONS:

Try making a diamond quilt wall hanging or tablecloth using the Starmaker⑧ for the center diamond. This will give you a longer, narrower design.

If you use the Starmaker⑤ for the center diamond, the diamond will be shorter and wider.

AMISH SILHOUETTE WALLHANGING

Finished size: 38" × 38"

Fabric needed: see below.

Binding: ⅓ yard

Fatt Batt™

This wallhanging has a reversible silhouette applique as its center motif. The floral silhouette is repeated in the outside corner blocks. On one side of this wall hanging, you may want to use the traditional solid Amish colors; while the other side could be made entirely of printed fabrics.

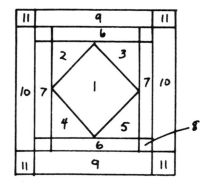

FABRIC REQUIREMENTS

Center Square (1)	Side A	13" × 13" square
	Side B	13" × 13" square
	Batting	13" × 13" square
Triangles (2,3,4,5)	Side A	1 piece 9½" × 20"
	Side B	1 piece 9½" × 20"
	Batting	1 piece 9½" × 20"
Narrow borders (6,7)	Side A	4 strips 3" × 18"
	Side B	4 strips 3" × 18"
	Batting	2 strips 3" × 18", cut lengthwise
		2 strips 3" × 24", cut lengthwise
Small squares (8)	Side A	1 strip 3" × 13"
	Side B	1 strip 3" × 13"
Wide borders (9,10)	Side A	4 strips 7" × 23"
	Side B	4 strips 7" × 23"
	Batting	2 strips 7" × 23", cut lengthwise
		2 strips 7" × 37", cut lengthwise
Large squares (11)	Side A	1 strip 7" × 28"
	Side B	1 strip 7" × 28"
Silhouette Applique	Side A	13" × 13" square
	Side B	13" × 13" square
Binding	⅓ yard	4 strips 3" × 45"

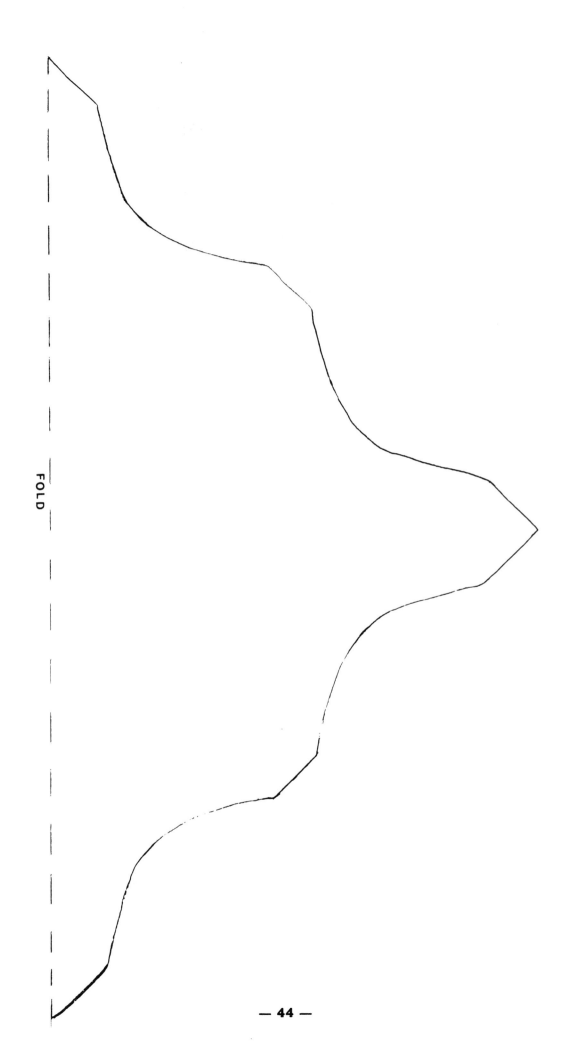

Step 1: Make a chart showing the colors you plan to use for each side of this wall hanging:

Side A	Position #	Side B
_____	1 (center square)	_____
_____	2,3,4,5 (triangles)	_____
_____	6,7 (narrow borders)	_____
_____	8 (small squares)	_____
_____	9,10 (wide borders)	_____
_____	11 (large squares)	_____
_____	Silhouette applique	_____

Write in the colors you plan to use for each position.

Step 2: Make a quilt sandwich from the squares in position #1: Side B square wrong side up; quilt batting square; Side A wrong side down.

Pin the three layers together carefully matching all sides. Zigzag the edges together.

Step 3: Do the Silhouette Applique in the center of the square. The square will be set into the quilt "on point." Follow the instructions for Silhouette Applique given in the chapter on Reversible Applique in this book.

Step 4: Cut a 9½" × 20" piece for Side A triangles.
Cut a 9½" × 20" piece for Side B triangles.
Mark the Side A piece on the right side of the fabric as shown.

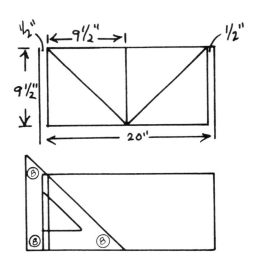

Starting at the left, mark a line at ½" from the end.

Draw a diagonal line from the top of the ½" line down to the bottom of the piece.

(Using the Starmaker⑧ to mark this diagonal line will insure the accuracy you need. Just line the bottom of the Starmaker along the bottom of the piece of fabric. Place the Starmaker so it goes off the top of the fabric just at the point where the ½" line is drawn.

Draw a vertical line on the piece of fabric. It should line up with the bottom of the first diagonal line.

Draw a second diagonal line going in the opposite direction. The Starmaker⑧ will give you a more accurate marking line.

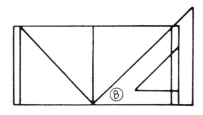

Then draw another vertical line from the top of the second diagonal line.

(Drawing the vertical lines at each end of this piece of fabric will insure a straight edge to the cut pieces.)

DO **NOT** CUT THE FABRIC!

Pin Side A and Side B fabric with wrong sides together. Pin on both sides of every marked line. The marked Side A should be facing up.

Cut the marked lines. DO NOT REMOVE THE PINS.

Each set of triangles pinned together will be the Side A and Side B which will be joined to the center square at the same time.

(MARKING AND CUTTING TRIANGLES IN THIS WAY WILL ALWAYS INSURE THAT THE GRAIN LINES RUN IN THE SAME DIRECTION IN EACH OF THE FOUR TRIANGLES ON ONE SIDE.)

Cut four triangles from the quilt batting.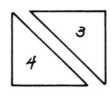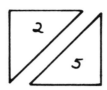

Step 5: Take the Position #2 triangles and one quilt batt triangle.

Place the Side B triangle with right side against the right side of the B center square. The long edge of the triangle must be along the edge of the center square.

Place the Side A triangle with right side against the right side of the A center square.

Lay the quilt batt triangle underneath the B triangle.

Pin all three layers together.

(ARE THE TRIANGLES PINNED TO THE UPPER LEFT CORNER OF THE SIDE A CENTER SQUARE?)

Sew with ¼" seam allowance. Open out the triangular piece. Pin and zigzag the open edges.

Add the triangles in positions #3, #4, and #5 in the same way.

Check the outside measurements of the finished square. It should measure 18" x 18". Trim the edges a little, if necessary.

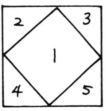

Step 6: Add the top and bottom border, position #6.

Strip B — right side against B center square.
Quilt batting strip — underneath Strip B.
Strip A — right side against A center square.

Pin carefully. Stitch with ¼" seam allowance.

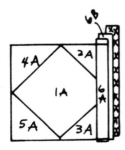 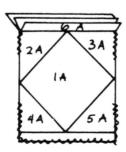

Open out the strip and batting.

Pin the edges together. Zigzag the edges.

Step 7: Mark the Side A strip for the small squares (position #8) into 3" squares.

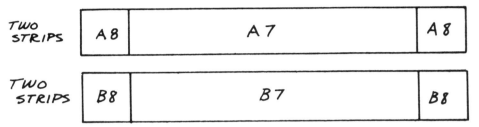

You will need four squares.

Pin the A strip and the B strip together with the marked side of the A strip on top. Pin on both sides of each marked line.

Cut on the marked lines; DO NOT REMOVE PINS.

Step 8: Sew one A square (position #8) to each end of the two remaining strips from position #7, Side A.

Sew one B square (position #8) to each end of the two remaining strips from position #7, Side B.

| TWO STRIPS | A8 | A7 | A8 |
| TWO STRIPS | B8 | B7 | B8 |

Lay the B strip (#7 and #8) with right sides against the center B. Place one 3" x 24" quilt batting strip underneath the B strip.

Place the A strip (#7 and #8) with right sides against the center A.

Pin carefully. Make sure the seam lines between #7 and #8 line up with the seam lines between the center square and #6.

Stitch with ¼" seam allowance. Open up the strips.

Pin the edges together. Zigzag.

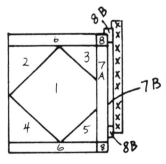 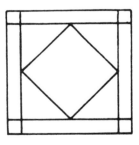

Step 9: Add the wide border strips (#9) in the same way the narrow strips were added in Step 6.

Step 10: Sew the large squares (#11) to each end of the wide borders (#10) the same way as in Step 8.

Step 11: Attach the binding to the wallhanging.

Step 12: Silhouette Applique in large corner blocks. Pin the material and the batting together carefully. Follow the instructions in Chapter III for Reversible Applique.

CHAPTER III
REVERSIBLE APPLIQUE

Several types of Reversible Applique can be used to add interest to reversible quilts. Reversible Applique is done on both Side A and Side B at the same time. There are three types of reversible applique that we will be covering here: Silhouette Applique, Broderie Perse, and Silhouette Quilting.

SILHOUETTE APPLIQUE: Silhouette applique is more effective when done in a dark solid colored fabric. Choose simple patterns because only the shape will identify the pattern. Shapes from coloring books, simplified animal shapes, some flowers and butterflies are easily identified by their outline. Paper cuttings and some Hawaiian quilting designs will work well. To determine if the pattern is suitable, cut out the design in block paper — can you tell what the design is without added details? Then it is suitable for Silhouette Applique. Several designs are included here that work well.

Step 1: If your reversible applique is to be placed in the center block, just finish the center block: zigzag together Side A, quilt batting, Side B. If the reversible applique is to be placed somewhere else in the quilt, finish the quilted item as far as necessary to do the applique. It is much easier to do the applique before the quilt is completely finished because there is less material to have to maneuver around, although it can be done after if necessary.

Step 2: Pin baste or hand baste the finished square where you will put the applique. I prefer to pin baste in two diagonal lines, one vertical line and one horizontal line, as shown. That seems to be enough to keep the fabrics from puckering.

Step 3: Cut two pieces of applique fabric. These may be the same color or two different colors. Make them at least 3 inches larger than your applique pattern.

Put iron-on interfacing on the back of each applique piece.

Pin one applique fabric with the wrong side against the Side A fabric; the other with the wrong side against the Side B fabric.

Step 4: Draw the silhouette design on a tear-away stabilizer or on a new product, called "Aqua-Solv." The design may be ironed on to either of these products or drawn on with a permanent marker or quilt marking pen.

Step 5: Set your machine for a straight stitch and a short (16-18) stitch length. Use either a regular presser foot, an applique foot, an embroidery foot, or an embroidery spring. If you use the regular or applique presser foot, loosen the pressure on the foot so the fabric can be turned easily under the foot without lifting the foot. I prefer to use an embroidery foot or spring because I can do the whole design without turning the fabric, which completely reduces the chances for puckers on the underneath fabric. With the feed mechanism lowered, you can move the fabric frontward, backward and side to side.

Step 6: Pin the silhouette design to Side A on top of the applique fabric. Use thread which contrasts with the applique fabric. This thread will not be visible when the applique is finished, but the contrast is necessary so you can trim close to the stitching line.

Stitch around the outline of the applique; also stitch around any inside design lines which you want to emphasize.

Remove the pattern. Excess "Aqua-Solv" can be removed by spraying with water. It will dissolve.

Trim the applique fabric close to the stitching lines on both sides.

Step 7: Set your machine for a medium wide zigzag, short (16-18) stitch length. Raise the feed mechanism, if it has been lowered. Loosen the pressure on the presser foot. Make sure your tension is balanced in the middle of the fabric. (Usually, when doing a satin stitch around an applique, the top tension should be loosened. But, because we need to finish an applique on both sides at the same time, we need to have a balanced tension.) You might want to try a sample satin stitch on a scrap of fabric which is the same thickness and density as your finished quilt square. Use a foot for your machine which has a grooved bottom to ride over the ridge of the satin stitch. Use thread on top and in the bobbin to match the applique fabric.

Begin satin stitching in the middle of a curved or straight line, never at a corner or point. There is no need to lock your beginning stitches; when finishing your satin stitching, sew over the beginning for a few stitches, then lock the ending stitches by changing your machine to a straight stitch and taking several stitches in one place.

Step 8: Any design lines within the pattern should be done with a satin stitch just wide enough to cover the contrasting thread.

BRODERIE PERSE: A pretty printed fabric, or fabric you have stencilled, may be used for one side of the applique; the reverse side of the applique will be a silhouette. To see if the print is suitable, make a black paper pattern of the outline. If you can tell what the pattern is, then the print is suitable, Or, the black pattern cut-out might look like an interesting free-form design. Either way, the design would be suitable. There are several fabrics with printed butterflies; try the bright children prints — cars, trucks, farm animals. Look for flowers which have very definite shapes.

Both the printed fabric and the silhouette fabric need to have iron-on interfacing on the back. Leave the edge around the printed fabric until after you do the straight stitching. In this case, the design is the print on the fabric; no tear-away or Aqua-Solv is necessary.

SILHOUETTE QUILTING: In silhouette quilting, a pieced patchwork design is made into Side A of the quilted item. After the block is finished, quilting is done around the design within the pieced block. Only the quilting shows on Side B. Patterns which have definite shapes within the block give the most pleasing quilting designs, such as star patterns, Grandmother's Flower Garden, and other geometric designs.

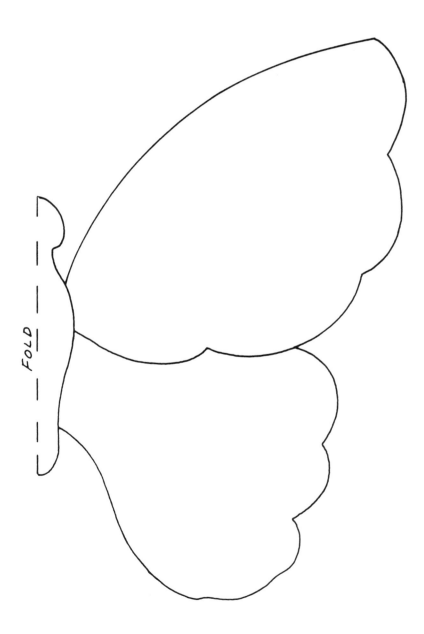

CHAPTER IV
REVERSIBLE CLOTHING

Vests, jackets, capes and wrap skirts may all be made reversible. This will really give you change-about wardrobe pieces. For vests and jackets, keep in mind that you will be adding bulk by having two layers and quilt batting. You may want to buy a larger size pattern. You may also want to eliminate the batting when using velvets or other heavy fabric.

One of my favorite fabric combinations is velvet or ultrasuede with a silky woven fabric. Try shades of faded denim reversed with red and white gingham or a red bandanna print.

Both sides of the reversible clothing will be finished at the same time and in the same manner as the quilts in this book.

Step 1: Make a heavy paper pattern of the complete garment (no fold lines or half patterns). Cut the first strips a little longer than the paper pattern. Place Side A strip with wrong side against the strip of quilt batt; place Side B strip on the other side of the batting with wrong side against the batt. Zigzag both long sides of the strips to hold them together. There is no need to zigzag the ends of the strips; these will be cut to the garment shape later.

Step 2: Add strips for Side A, Side B, and strips of quilt batting to these first strips. If you are not sure how to do this, read Chapter I. After several strips have been added, lay the sewn together strips down on the paper pattern. Trim the ends; but it is a good idea to leave an extra inch on both the top and bottom of the strips.

Step 3: After all of the pattern pieces are finished, sew them with Side A's together. Enclose the seam allowances on Side B by laying a 1½" strip right side down even with the raw edges of the pattern pieces. Sew at ¼". Fold the strip over the seam allowance; turn under the raw edge; pin the folded edge just to the seam allowance. Topstitch by machine or blind stitch by hand through just the seam allowance.

VESTS — If the pattern and design have simple lines, cut the vest front and back without side seams. This would be possible in the following designs.

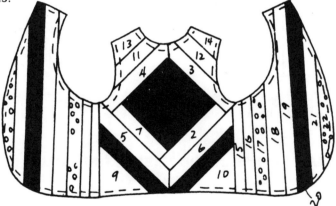

The back would be done first with the pieces added in the numbered sequence; then starting at the side seam, the strips would be added until the center fronts matched the paper pattern.

If side seams are necessary, such as for the following designs, then both the side seams and the shoulder seams will need to be enclosed.

A-LINE WRAP SKIRTS — Angle the strips so they line up with the side seams. To do this, make the strips wider at the bottom than at the top; usually just ½" to 1" wider on each strip will give you the results you want. Enclose the side seams; bind all the outside edges. Add a waistband or bind the waist.

JACKETS — Make a paper pattern all in one piece by pinning the shoulder seams together; leave the side seams and the sleeve seam open. Pin the sleeves to the armhole. Your pattern will now look like this:

After sewing all of the reversible pieces, sew the underarm and sleeve seams. Enclose the seam allowances. Bind the outside edges of the jacket.

TRY THESE JACKET DESIGNS:

Make these jackets all in one piece; then cut out the neckhole and center front after the piecing is all done.

Do the vertical pieces for the front and back first; then do the horizontal sleeve pieces. One of the horizontal seams will have to be enclosed.

TRY THESE VARIATIONS IN YOUR REVERSIBLE CLOTHING:

1. Use short scraps for the strips. Cut them all the same width; but vary the length. This is very effective with ultrasuede scraps. Sew the scraps together into longer strips before using them in your clothing.

2. In the center of the back or in the back shoulder area, do a Reversible Silhouette Applique. The directions for this type of applique are found in Chapter III.

3. On Side A, piece a geometric patchwork pattern, such as Grandmother's Flower Garden or Tumbling Blocks. After placing Side A, Side B, and the quilt batt together, machine quilt around the pieced design. Just the quilting will show on Side B, so check to see that the quilting will form an interesting pattern.

CHAPTER V

HOW TO FINISH A QUILT

QUILT PLANNING

In planning the quilt, we have to consider the different parts of the quilt top.

Main part — centered from foot of bed to the tuck under the pillow.

    The main part can be made up of many quilt squares or one large quilt square.

    The quilt squares from the main part should not drop over the edge of the bed.

Drop — The drop is the area from the top of the mattress to the floor on two sides and the foot.

    If you don't want the quilt to go to the floor, measure the distance from the top of the mattress to the desired length.

    The drop can have another row of quilt blocks, partial quilt block patterns, or decorative borders.

Borders — The borders on the quilt serve as a frame. It should highlight the colors in the quilt and even repeat the colors within the quilt blocks.

    Several borders may be added to the quilt top, but the borders should not overpower the main part of the quilt top.

Binding — The binding serves as a narrow border. It also finishes the edges of the quilt. On some types of quilts, the binding is eliminated.

Mattress Sizes:

    Crib — 27" x 52"
    Twin — 39" x 75"
    Full — 54" x 75"
    Queen — 60" x 80"
    King — 72" x 84"

Waterbeds depend on the type. Some take the same size quilt as a traditional bed. Others have frames and the quilts need less of a drop because the quilt will be tucked into the frame.

Other things to consider in determining the quilt size:

    If the quilts will come up and over the pillows, add 15" to 20" for this. This may equal the amount added in borders and the drop at the foot of the bed; just add the same amount to foot and pillow end of the bed.

    Add several extra inches in the length and width. The quilting will take up the inches.

YARDAGE NEEDED

    For an exact yardage amount, take a look at *Taking the Math Out of Making Patchwork Quilts*, by Bonnie Leman and Judy Martin, or *The Quick Quiltmaking Handbook* by Barbara Johannah.

    For a close estimate of the yardage needed, take the total needed for a quilt top; divide it by the number of colors planned. For reversible quilts, buy twice the amount of fabric.

        Twin bed — 6 yards
        Full — 8 yards
        Queen — 10 yards
        King — 12 yards

    If two colors are used, divide the total by 2. If the main color is used for more than half of the design, I buy an extra yard of that color.

    This method is good for me because I like to have extra fabric left after a project is finished.

TYING YOUR QUILT

    Quilts may be tied by hand or machine instead of being quilted. The ties hold the three layers (front, back and batting) together.

To tie your quilt by machine, first pin your quilt together near each spot you will put a tie. Ties are usually put in the center of each quilt square or at the corners of the quilt blocks. Other quilts may have the ties evenly divided all over the top of the quilt.

Ties are usually yarn, but can be rickrack, trims, or cording. If the quilt is to be washed, the yarn should be washable. Use thread in the top and bottom that matches the yarn. Lay the yarn on top of the quilt. Lower the feed mechanism on your machine. Set your machine for a wide zigzag stitch. Zigzag over the yarn several times. Lockstitch by changing to a straight stitch and taking several stitches. With the feed mechanism lowered, the stitches will form a bartack.

Bartack   Tie the yarn in a bow.

BORDERS

Size: The width of the border should relate to the size of the quilt blocks and sashing between blocks.

When several borders are added, the first border may be narrower to give depth to the design of the quilt. Using a narrow dark first border will add even more depth.

If borders need to be pieced, the seam line between pieces should be placed in the center; two seams should be divided evenly. A square of contrasting fabric can be added where the seam lines meet.

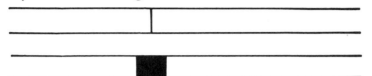

The border may also be made up of parts of the design used in the quilt blocks.

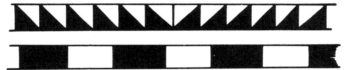

If the main part of the quilt is a very busy pattern, at least the first border should be a solid color. Striped fabric can make a very effective border.

Borders may be squared off at the corners. Top and bottom borders are added; then the two side borders are added. This is sometimes referred to as "log cabin" method of adding borders.

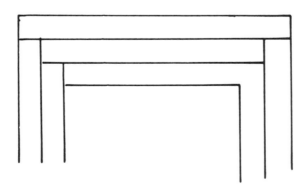

BINDINGS

Bindings finish off the edges of quilts. The binding may be a separate straight or bias strip, or the backing of the quilt may be folded around to the front to form a binding.

If the backing is to form the binding, the backing fabric must be cut 3" or 4" larger all around.

If the edges of the quilt are straight, I prefer a binding cut on the straight of grain. It is much easier to handle and takes much less fabric and time. If the edges are rounded, a bias binding must be used.

Straight binding — A double or French fold binding will lay much smoother and last longer than a single fold.

Finished Binding	Cut Strip
½"	3"
1"	6"
1½"	9"

Fold the binding strip in half lengthwise, wrong sides together. I use Verna Holt's tip for folding and pressing the fabric at the same time.

Stick a long needle or corsage pin into the ironing board cover. The pin should just cover the folded strip. Place an iron to the right of the pin. Pull the strip under the pin and under the iron. It will come out folded and pressed perfectly.

HOW MUCH BINDING DO YOU NEED?

Add two times the length of your quilt,
two times the width of your quilt,
plus one extra foot (just in case)
2 x l + 2 x w + 12"

To apply the binding. First, machine baste with a wide zigzag the outside edges of the quilt, batt and backing.

The binding is sewn to either Side A or Side B. Both raw edges of the binding should be placed even with the outside edges of the quilt.

Sew the binding to the quilt with the same seam allowance as the finished binding. If the finished binding is one inch, the seam allowance should be one inch.

Fold the binding to the opposite side; pin in place. The folded edge should come in the same distance from the edge as the seam allowance. Pin the folded edge. Blind stitch by hand.

Lapped Binding. In a lapped binding, the binding is attached to two opposite edges of the quilt. Then it is attached to the two remaining edges; tuck the edges in, then topstitch. The edges that are tucked in should be hand stitched to keep them from coming out.

Continuous Binding. Do not start at a corner; instead start along one of the sides. Start stitching about 4 inches from the end of the strip. Just leave the 4 inches unsewn. Sew to the corner with binding side up.

DIRECTIONS FOR LAPPED BINDING:

Fold and press the binding strips in half lengthwise, with wrong sides together.
Pin the folded binding strip with the long raw edges even with the raw edges of the quilt.
Sew the strips to both sides of the quilt.

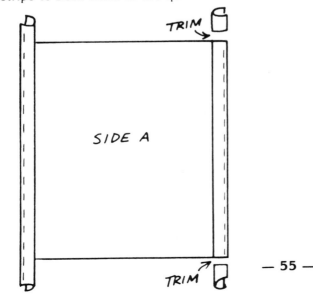

Trim binding ends even with the edges of the quilt.

Bring folded edge of binding to reverse side of quilt.

Pin in place. Blind stitch by hand, or top stitch by machine.

Pin a folded binding strip to the top and bottom of the quilt. The binding strip should extend ½ inch on both ends.

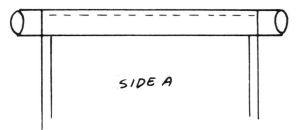

Sew ¼ inch seam allowance.

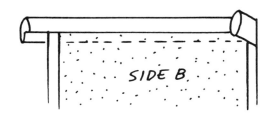

Open out the binding strip.
Fold the ½" extension on each side in. It will cover the seam allowance of the quilt and binding.

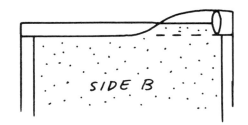

Bring folded edge of binding to reverse side of quilt.
Pin in place.
Blind stitch by hand or topstitch by machine.

Mitered Corner Binding. Mark a point the width of seam allowance from both edges on the quilt back. Place a pin at the outside edge in line with the marked point. Sew to the marked point (the pin will serve as a guide). The stitching must end right at the point. Lockstitch.

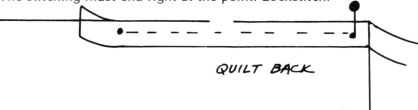

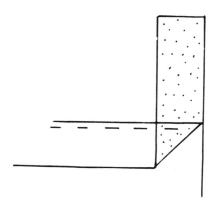

Fold the binding strip up at right angles.

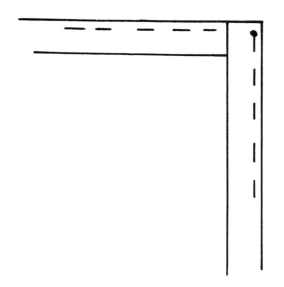

Bring the binding down with the corner square. (This forms a pleat.) Put the needle down into the same point where you ended your stitching. Lock stitches.

Sew to the next corner.

Repeat.

When you come within a few inches of the beginning of the strip, fold back ½" of the beginning edge of the strip. Lay the end of the strip on top of the beginning. Cut the end even with the folded back ½" of the beginning.

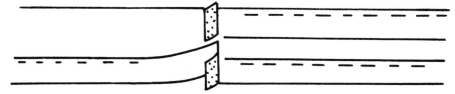

Bring the two ends of the binding right side together. Sew the short ends together with ¼" seam allowance. The ends of the binding should now be seamed, with no overlapping edges.

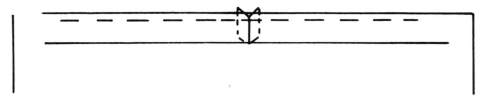

Continue sewing this part of the binding to the quilt back.

Fold the binding to the front; pin in place. The corners will form a mitre by tucking one part of the binding under the other. The diagonal fold can be hand stitched in place, or left unsewn; after the edge of the binding is topstitched, the fold will stay in place.

Topstitch binding.

HOW TO MAKE CONTINUOUS STRAIGHT BINDING:

Mark along the length of the fabric a cutting line the width of the binding strip needed.

Finished Binding	Cut Width
½"	3"
1"	6"
1½"	9"

Bring the two ends right sides together; match A to A, etc. The first marked width will be offset one strip. Sew the ends. Press seams open.

Begin cutting the marked strips. Cut continuously until the whole piece of fabric is cut.

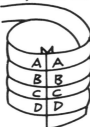

1 yard of 45" wide fabric will give you 13 yards of continuous straight binding, when the binding is 3" wide.

Robbie Fanning, in her book *The Complete Book of Machine Quilting*, has much more information on all types of bindings for quilts.

HOW TO MAKE CONTINUOUS BIAS BINDING:

Cut one square of fabric.
Mark the diagonal line.
Cut on the diagonal line.

Sew triangle A to the other side of triangle B.
Press seam allowances open.

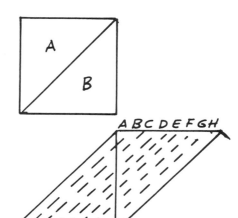

Mark cutting lines the width desired.
Measure the distance from the diagonal edge.

Finished binding
    ½" — cut strip 3" wide
    1" — cut strip 6" wide
    1½" — cut strip 9" wide
Bring right sides together; offset one strip.

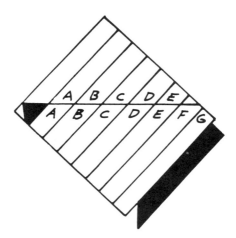

Begin cutting at either end; cut continuously until the whole piece of fabric is cut.

OTHER TYPES OF QUILT FINISHES

PRAIRIE POINTS:

Prairie points make a very effective edge for any type of quilt or wallhanging. The traditional method to make prairie points is to cut squares of fabric (3, 4, 5, or even 6 inches square).

Fold the squares diagonally.

Then fold diagonally in the other direction.

Press.

The folded edge of one triangle slips halfway inside the open folded edge of the next triangle.

Stitch along raw edge of all the triangles.

Prairie Points are sewn to just one side of quilt top; raw edge of prairie points even with raw edge of quilt.

Fold under the edge of the reverse side of the quilt. Pin. Blind stitch by hand or topstitch by machine.

PRAIRIE POINTS (fast method) —

Step 1: Cut a 4½" × 45" strip of fabric.

Mark the strip with line ½" from one long edge.

Mark the strip every 4 inches vertically.

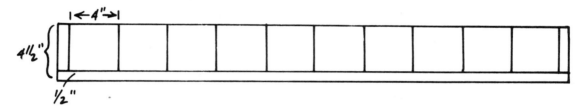

Cut on the vertical lines (only down to the horizontal line).

Step 2: Fold and press each section diagonally.

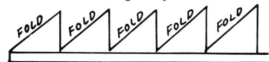

Fold and press each section diagonally in the other direction.

Step 3: Topstitch along the bottom of the folded triangles, just catching the raw edges.

This will give you a nice sawtooth edge.

I learned this technique from Lu Rae Barlow, owner of LuRae's Creative Stitchery, through the **"Stitchery Garden,"** a newsletter of the National Machine Embroidery Guild.

To make Prairie Points look like the traditional Prairie Points, follow Steps 1 and 2 above.

Step 3: Cut another 4½" × 45". This can be the same fabric or a coordinating fabric.

Mark this strip the same way.

Cut on vertical lines (only down to the horizontal line).

Step 4: Fold and press each section diagonally.

CAUTION: Notice that the diagonal fold is in the opposite direction for this strip.

Fold and press each section diagonally in the other direction.

Step 5: Place the two strips with the marked ½" horizontal lines together.

Bring the bottom raw edge of the underneath strip on top of the top strip.

one side

Bring the raw edge at the bottom of the triangle of the top strip underneath the bottom strip.

opposite side

Pin bottom edges in place.

Topstitch close to the raw edges at the bottom of the triangles.

The ½" strip at the bottom of the triangles goes into the seam allowance of the quilt.

Pin the strip to the edge of Side A.

Stitch at about ⅝" from the raw edge of strip and quilt top.

Fold under the edge of Side B. Pin. Blind stitch by hand or topstitch by machine.